THE
BIRD SONGS
— ANTHOLOGY —

THE
BIRD SONGS
— ANTHOLOGY —

200 BIRDS FROM NORTH AMERICA AND BEYOND

by Les Beletsky

CHRONICLE BOOKS

SAN FRANCISCO

Copyright © 2007 by becker&mayer!
Patent Pending.

The credits that appear on page 363 are hereby made a part of this copyright page.

Library of Congress Control Number: 2007927076

ISBN: 1-932855-88-2
ISBN-13: 978-1-932855-88-3

The Bird Songs Anthology: 200 Birds from North America and Beyond
is produced by becker&mayer!, Bellevue, Washington.
www.beckermayer.com

Front cover illustrations: David Nurney (Eastern Yellow Wagtail, Lilac-breasted Roller,
Scarlet Tanager, and New Zealand Kaka) and Mike Langman (Whistling Fruit Dove)

Back cover illustrations: David Nurney (Scarlet Minivets and Streamer-tailed Tyrant)
and John Sill (Olive Warbler)

Audio Editing: Kate Hall
Custom Audio Engineering: Steve Beck
Design: Henry Quiroga
Editorial: Meghan Cleary and Kate Perry
Production Coordination: Leah Finger
Product Development: Peter Schumacher
Project Management: Sheila Kamuda
Track Descriptions: Gerrit Vyn

10 9 8 7 6 5 4 3 2 1

Printed and manufactured in China

Chronicle Books LLC
680 Second Street
San Francisco, CA 94107

www.chroniclebooks.com

TABLE OF CONTENTS

FOREWORD

One hundred and fifty years ago, Passenger Pigeons still migrated by the hundreds of millions over the eastern United States twice each year. Tens of thousands of Eskimo Curlews descended on New England blueberry fields each fall, and on black-earth prairies of the Great Plains each spring. Had there been a conservation-minded laboratory dedicated to ornithology back then, we might still be seeing spectacular flocks of these now-extinct birds today. In its largest sense, the Cornell Lab's fundamental mission is simple, and dates back to the era when humans first recognized the fundamental importance of birds as windows into the natural world: We interpret and conserve the earth's precious natural areas and species, their processes and interactions, and their evolutionary potential.

We accomplish our mission by studying, teaching about, conserving, and celebrating the earth's most beautiful and powerful messengers of nature. By connecting us so powerfully with nature, birds help us understand how the natural world functions and what it requires to persist in the face of change. We study endangered birds to keep them from going extinct, and just as importantly, we study our backyard birds in order to keep common birds common. Ultimately, we seek to maintain the underlying natural systems upon which all our birds depend. This is the essence of conservation.

The Cornell Laboratory of Ornithology is unique in the world. Every day we unite internationally recognized scientists with students of all ages and citizens of all occupations. We embrace and cherish the notion that science is not an exercise for the ivory tower; it is simply an organized way of being curious about how nature works. Everybody is born with this curiosity, and we can share our explorations with millions of citizens around the world, helping them enjoy the wonders of our living planet. At the same time that we provide resources to help people explore, we also seek the knowledge that emerges from countless observations in backyards, neighborhood parks, school grounds, cemeteries, and woodlots.

We are pleased to be a partner in the production of *The Bird Songs Anthology*, which uses sounds from our Macaulay Library, the world's largest archive of animal sounds and animal behavior videos. This collection was built on the premise that the more people understand bird song and bird behavior, the more they will act to protect birds and the precious environment we all share. It is our fondest wish that these songs and images will inspire you to learn more about birds and take a more active role in their conservation, both with the Lab and elsewhere. For more information, I invite you to visit our Web site at www.birds.cornell.edu.

With my thanks and wishes for good birding,

Dr. John Fitzpatrick
Louis Agassiz Fuertes Executive Director
Cornell Lab of Ornithology

INTRODUCTION

Birdwatchers and other wildlife enthusiasts can easily spot familiar birds every day, but the birds that inhabit far-flung lands are much harder to view. Many enthusiasts dream of traveling to foreign regions to see birds both common and rare, and to hear their unfamiliar songs and calls. They are curious about such charming, celebrated groups as the noisy toucans of South America, the amazing hornbills of Africa and Asia, the secretive kiwis of New Zealand, the song-mimicking lyrebirds of Australia, and many others. Now, with this book, bird lovers can explore at leisure some of the sights and sounds of birds around the globe.

We selected two hundred of the world's most interesting bird species for *The Bird Songs Anthology*. Some represent families strongly associated with particular continents; others are especially striking, attractive, or rare. A beautiful full-color painting by talented artists David Nurney or Mike Langman accompanies each selection, along with a concise description of the bird's behavior, environment, and vocalizations. On the remarkable built-in digital audio player, you will hear each bird as it sings or calls in nature.

The audio recordings of the birds presented here were provided by the Macaulay Library at the Cornell Lab of Ornithology, which maintains recordings of more than 160,000 natural sounds, including sixty-seven percent of the world's birds.

USING THE COLLECTION

The Bird Songs Anthology is divided into six chapters, each devoted to a different continent. Only Antarctica is not covered, because it has few bird species.

The chapters begin with a brief account of the continent's characteristic birds, along with a captivating landscape painting by Mike Langman that shows several of the birds covered in the chapter in their natural environment. The habitats pictured include a western Mexico woodland, a streamside Brazilian rainforest, a grassy plain in Europe, a savanna woodland in Africa, a wet tropical forest in Asia, and a eucalyptus woodland in Australasia. The information about bird sounds presented in this book requires a bit of explanation. There are two general types of bird vocalizations: songs and calls. "Songs" are usually considered longer, often more melodic vocalizations; "calls" are typically briefer and nonmusical. For instance, the Australian Golden Whistler, which lives in Australia and New Guinea, has a song that sounds like a *peep-peep-peep-peep-pu-wit*, whereas its frequently uttered call sounds like a *seep*. One school of thought among bird experts is that true bird songs are largely restricted to the more recently evolved birds, called songbirds, which have more complex sound-producing apparatus in their respiratory passages. Most of the small birds that many of us recognize are these advanced birds, such as wrens, thrushes, jays, warblers, blackbirds, sparrows, and finches.

In addition, experts sometimes define songs as the vocalizations male birds use to advertise their territories to possible mates and male competitors; these are called "advertising songs" or "territorial songs." Calls, on the other hand, are not used to attract mates and discourage competitors; rather, they are audio signals that serve a variety of other purposes. For example, birds utter calls as alarm signals, alerting other birds of predators, and to foster interactions between mates or between adults and young. Birds also frequently give short calls to keep in contact with members of their flock.

For birdwatchers and other nature lovers, looking at and listening to the spectacular birds in *The Bird Songs Anthology* will be a thrilling experience.

—*Les Beletsky*

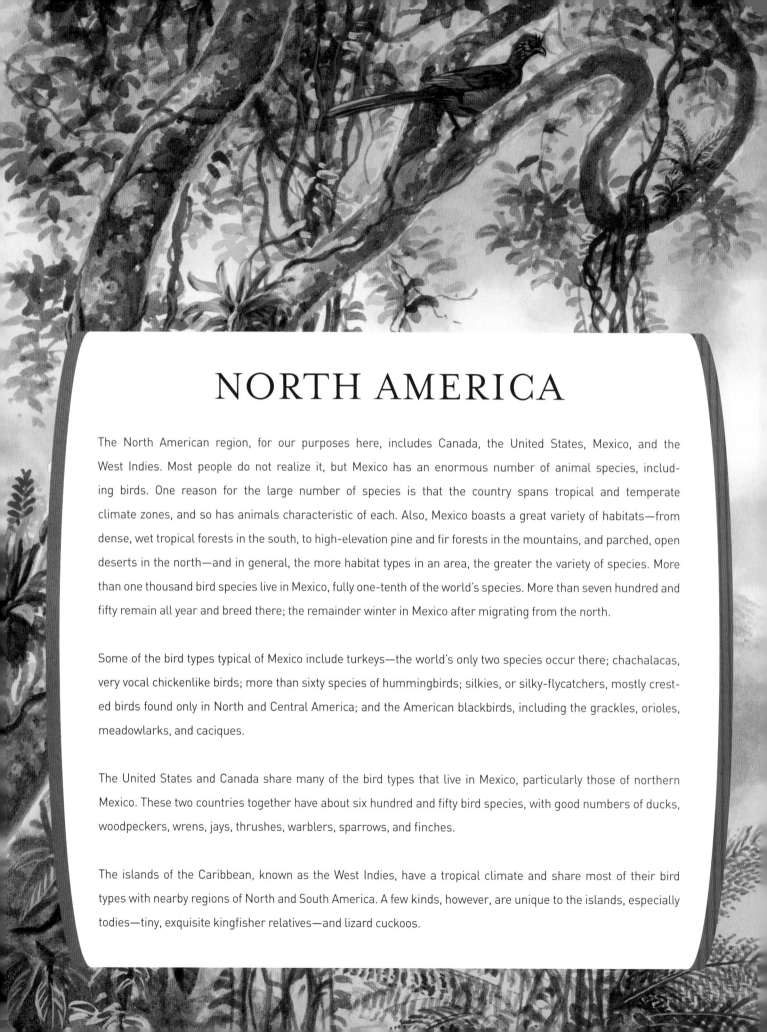

NORTH AMERICA

The North American region, for our purposes here, includes Canada, the United States, Mexico, and the West Indies. Most people do not realize it, but Mexico has an enormous number of animal species, including birds. One reason for the large number of species is that the country spans tropical and temperate climate zones, and so has animals characteristic of each. Also, Mexico boasts a great variety of habitats—from dense, wet tropical forests in the south, to high-elevation pine and fir forests in the mountains, and parched, open deserts in the north—and in general, the more habitat types in an area, the greater the variety of species. More than one thousand bird species live in Mexico, fully one-tenth of the world's species. More than seven hundred and fifty remain all year and breed there; the remainder winter in Mexico after migrating from the north.

Some of the bird types typical of Mexico include turkeys—the world's only two species occur there; chachalacas, very vocal chickenlike birds; more than sixty species of hummingbirds; silkies, or silky-flycatchers, mostly crested birds found only in North and Central America; and the American blackbirds, including the grackles, orioles, meadowlarks, and caciques.

The United States and Canada share many of the bird types that live in Mexico, particularly those of northern Mexico. These two countries together have about six hundred and fifty bird species, with good numbers of ducks, woodpeckers, wrens, jays, thrushes, warblers, sparrows, and finches.

The islands of the Caribbean, known as the West Indies, have a tropical climate and share most of their bird types with nearby regions of North and South America. A few kinds, however, are unique to the islands, especially todies—tiny, exquisite kingfisher relatives—and lizard cuckoos.

COMMON LOON

— *Gavia immer* —

((001))

The haunting wail, or wolf's howl, of a Common Loon.

Some of the world's most beautiful waterbirds, loons are divers specialized for foraging underwater. The Common Loon, which breeds on freshwater lakes in forests across northern North America, is the continent's best-known loon, owing to the extensive public concern over its declining populations and the environmental factors that threaten it. During breeding, Common Loons have black backs with large white patches.

The Common Loon's yodel—its territorial call, given only by the male—is called the "song of the loon." The birds produce these loud, long, haunting vocalizations during the breeding season, usually at night, often from the otherwise quiet lakes of northern New England, the northern Midwest, Canada, and Alaska. Yodels carry up to a mile, and each male's call is unique to that individual. Other calls of the Common Loon, given by both sexes, are a wail that sounds like a wolf's howl, a hoot, and a laughing call known as a tremolo. The Common Loon's wail is its most common call prior to nesting; yodels are most common during and after nesting. Loons give most calls at night, but some, mostly tremolos, they give during the day, in response to disturbances by humans or from other sources.

HORNED GREBE

— Podiceps auritus —

002

One of several trilling calls given by
Horned Grebes during the breeding season.

Horned Grebes are small members of the grebe family, fully aquatic diving birds often mistaken for ducks. They breed from Alaska through much of western and central Canada and northern Montana, North Dakota, and Minnesota. They winter along the Atlantic and Pacific coasts. Horned Grebes, which nest on small ponds and lake inlets, are intensely territorial. During breeding, they are a handsome reddish brown and black, with distinctive "horns"—golden yellow patches of feathers behind the eyes.

These grebes give a variety of calls, many of them trilling or chittering. Most calls are thought to relate to territorial defense or to establishing and maintaining the pair bond. Duet-trills, often given by members of a breeding pair when they meet, are loud, accelerating trills: *dji-ji-ji-ji ji-ji-jrrh*. Threat chitters, also given by both members of a pair, resemble duet-trills, but more staccato and stuttering: *kru-vu kru-vu kru-vu* or *dji-ji dji-ji dji-ji*. Advertising calls are loud and nasal: *aaanrrh* or *jaorrrh*, usually descending in pitch and ending in a rattle; lone individuals often give these calls at the beginning of pair formation.

NORTHERN FULMAR

— Fulmarus glacialis —

The cackling calls, repeated braying *aaark* notes, of a pair of fulmars at a nesting site.

The Northern Fulmar, another tube-nosed seabird related to albatrosses and pe-
trels, is abundant along the coasts of Alaska and the Canadian Arctic. Few people
see them from land in these regions, however, because they tend to remain off-
shore and breed only in a few remote places. Fulmars come in several color forms,
ranging from mostly white with a light gray back to uniformly dark brownish gray,
with every gradation in between. Renowned scavengers of waste generated by in-
dustrial fishing operations, fulmars also take a wide variety of fish and squid. They
are among the longest-lived birds, sometimes surviving for forty years or more.

Fulmars vocalize mainly while ashore—at or near nest sites—but sometimes
also while in flocks floating near food resources, and occasionally in flight.
Their main vocalizations, known as cackling, are rapid, braying *aaark* notes interspersed with rasping, breathy sounds: *AAARK-aaww-AAARK-aawww-AAARK*
or *cock-cock-cock-cock-aawww-cock-cock-cock*. Pairs cackle during courtship,
in territorial aggression against intruders, and when parents approach chicks;
single birds apparently cackle unprovoked. Other calls include short grunts,
which are inaudible beyond a few yards, and mewing sounds emitted when
fulmars are frightened.

MAGNIFICENT FRIGATEBIRD

— Fregata magnificens —

((004))

The noisy calls of a frigatebird given at a Florida breeding colony.

Frigatebirds are large, beautiful seabirds with huge, pointed wings and long, forked tails. A pleasure to watch as they soar silently along coastal areas, they occupy most of the world's tropical ocean regions. The Magnificent Frigatebird occurs along Mexico's coasts and, in the United States, mainly in Florida and along the Gulf Coast. Frigatebirds feed on the wing, swooping low to catch fish and pluck squid and jellyfish from the wavetops. However, these birds cannot swim and so do not rest on the water; they alight only on land, often on remote islands. Male frigatebirds have a large, red throat pouch that they inflate, balloonlike, during courtship displays.

The Magnificent Frigatebird is generally quiet during nonbreeding periods. Breeding colonies can be very noisy with courtship calls and an array of twittering, rattling, or whinnying sounds.

AMERICAN BITTERN

— Botaurus lentiginosus —

((🐦 005))

The deep, gulping, advertising song, *pump-er-lunk*, of the elusive American Bittern.

The American Bittern is a solitary, medium-sized heron that breeds in freshwater wetlands from the mid–United States to northern Canada. It prefers areas with tall, emergent vegetation, and within this habitat it frequents vegetation fringes and shorelines. Most active at dawn and dusk, American Bitterns are stealthy in their foraging, waiting motionless for long periods to capture passing insects, amphibians, and small fish and mammals.

This bittern uses vocalizations mainly to communicate within the thick vegetation that dominates its aquatic world. The calls heard most often during the breeding season are low and resonant, sometimes rendered as *pump-er-lunk* or *dunk-a-doo*. These calls are usually preceded by a series of clicking and gulping sounds, and they function primarily as territorial signals and as mate advertisements.

ANHINGA

— *Anhinga anhinga* —

The descending, rattling croaks of a perched Anhinga.

Anhingas, closely related to cormorants, are distinctive birds of fresh and brackish waters in the southeastern United States. They are large birds with very long, slim necks and long, sharply pointed bills, which they use to spear fish. Males are mostly black but have large patches of white on the wings; females are similar, but with light brown heads and necks. With their long necks, Anhingas are often called "snakebirds" because they sometimes swim with only their heads and necks above the water, looking startlingly like snakes gliding across the water's surface. A truly aquatic species, Anhingas spend their lives in water or on branches overhanging protected streams and ponds.

Away from the nest, Anhingas are generally silent, but they sometimes make clicking calls or shrill rattling sounds either in flight or from a perch. At the nest, these birds have a much wider vocal repertoire full of harsh croaks, rattles, and grunts. The most common call from both sexes is a distinctive, rapid, undulating clicking or chattering, sometimes rising then falling in pitch, that sounds a bit like a treadle-operated sewing machine. These vocalizations can transition into loud, harsh *cruk-cruk-cruks*, which are given frequently when one parent relieves the other for incubation duty at an egg-filled nest.

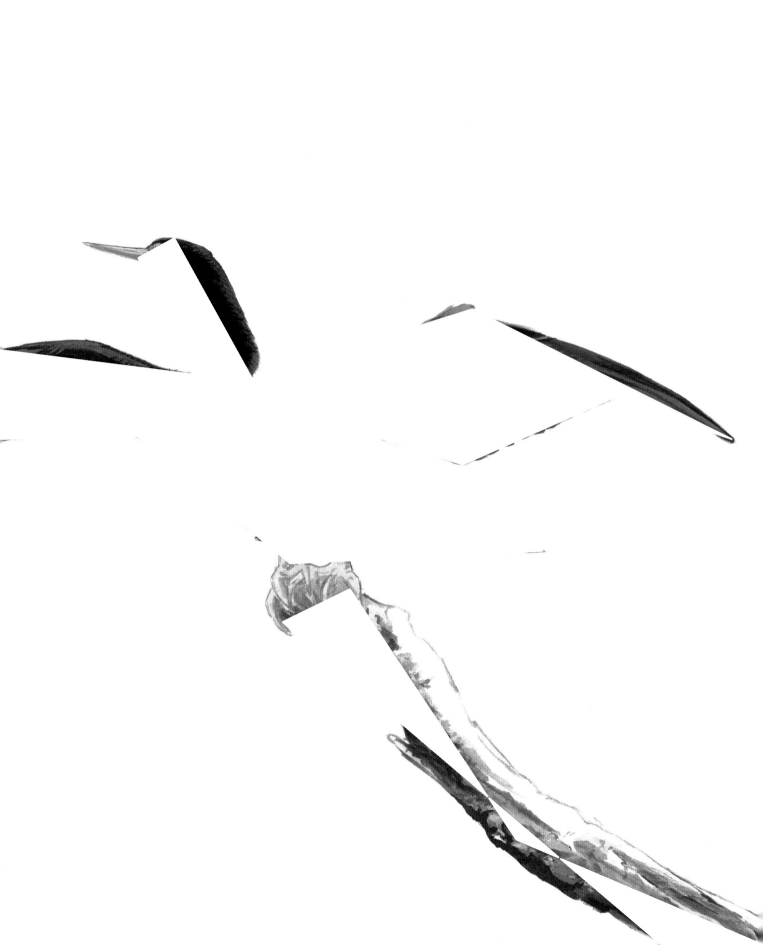

ROSEATE SPOONBILL

— Platalea ajaja —

The grunting alarm calls of a Roseate Spoonbill at a rookery.

One of North America's most unusual-looking wading birds, the Roseate Spoonbill is truly flamboyant, with a pink body, red on its wings and tail, a naked head, and a bill shaped like a spatula, which gives the bird its name. In the United States, spoonbills are found mainly in Florida and along the Gulf Coast, where they frequent shallow aquatic habitats, both inland and along the coast. The species also dwells along the Atlantic and Pacific coasts of Mexico and southward into South America. These striking birds feed in marine and freshwater areas, such as bays, estuaries, wet meadows, marshes, swamps, and mudflats. The spoonbill forages by walking along and swinging its head and the slightly open "spoon" of the bill from side to side in the water; the bill snaps shut when it touches prey—mainly fish, crustaceans, and insects. The spoonbill is gregarious while feeding, nesting, and roosting.

Roseate Spoonbills produce only a few vocalizations. The only sound uttered away from nesting areas is a soft, grunting *uh-uh-uh*, often heard during feeding. An alarm call, associated with breeding, sounds like *huh-huh-huh-huh*. When mates greet each other, and perhaps when they perform courtship displays, they produce low cackling, clucking, or croaking sounds.

TRUMPETER SWAN

— Cygnus buccinator —

((008))

The trumpeting *honks* of a breeding pair of swans.

The Trumpeter Swan is the largest native North American waterfowl. A long-lived, social species, it is eye-catching because of its large size, all-white plumage, and trumpetlike call. Formerly abundant and geographically widespread, European settlement of the continent greatly reduced its numbers and distribution, but the species has made a good recovery because of conservation efforts. Trumpeter Swans breed in localized regions of Alaska, western Canada, and the northern United States. They winter along Canada's western coast, the northwestern coast of the United States, and in isolated pockets of the western interior. Introduced populations now occur locally to the east of these regions in the Great Lakes area. Adult Trumpeter Swans eat aquatic vegetation, grasses, grains, some crop plants, and occasionally fish and fish eggs.

Trumpeter swans call year-round in a variety of situations, including when alone or in pairs or flocks, in flight, and when swimming or standing. The common name of the species, Trumpeter, is derived from its typical call, a honking *oh-OH* given in a variety of contexts, including confrontational encounters during territorial defense, when excited, and when alarmed. Other calls include peeps, hisses, and gurgles. Nesting Trumpeters are less vocal than nonbreeding individuals.

WOOD DUCK

— Aix sponsa —

((009))

A male's whistled contact call.

One of the globe's most gorgeous ducks, the Wood Duck is a common denizen of wooded swamps, freshwater marshes, and slow-moving rivers. The males, with their distinctive facial pattern and iridescent green and purple head, take high honors as beautiful waterbirds. The bodies of Wood Ducks are fairly slim, most likely because they nest not in coastal or marsh vegetation but in natural cavities with small openings, such as tree holes made by large woodpeckers. The species occurs in many of the contiguous forty-eight states and in southern Canada. It eats seeds, fruits, aquatic and terrestrial beetles, flies, snails, and other small animals.

The basic call of male Wood Ducks, used to keep individuals in contact, is a drawn-out whistle: *ji-ihb* or a low, squeaky *jeeb*. The male burp call, which consists of short *pfits* often linked together in a series, draws attention during courtship, but it is also used as a warning signal. Another male call is the nest-search call, *jib-jibjib*, which is used when females are searching for nest cavities and is thought to reinforce the pair bond. The female hauk call—a loud *oo-eek, oo-eek*—is perhaps the most familiar vocalization of Wood Ducks, often given when females take flight after being disturbed.

NORTHERN SHOVELER

— Anas clypeata —

((🐦))
010

A series of paired *took* calls by a male.

Common and widely distributed in North America, the Northern Shoveler is easily recognized by its elongated, spoonlike bill, which it uses as a foraging tool. To feed, these ducks hold their large bills in the water while they swim, straining out tiny aquatic animals such as crustaceans and insects, though they also eat seeds. They are found in a variety of wetland habitats, breeding from Alaska and central Canada east to the Great Lakes, and wintering in the western and southern United States. Like most ducks, male shovelers are more colorful than females, with green heads, white breasts, and brown sides.

These unusual-looking ducks give several different calls. The *took,* the most common male vocalization, is given in a variety of social situations. Another male call, produced frequently during fall and early winter but rarely at other times, sounds like *paaay . . . took-took . . . took-took*. Females give various quacks in different contexts. For instance, during the pairing season, females give short series of loud, evenly spaced, single quacks at dusk, but during the period immediately before egg-laying, females give long series of single quacks, and mated females being chased by males utter single loud quacks followed by quieter *gaek* notes.

COMMON MERGANSER

— Mergus merganser —

((011))

The female *gruk gruk gruk* call, often given by alarmed mergansers.

The Common Merganser is a large fish-eating diving duck that nests near lakes and rivers in northern forested habitats in North America, Europe, and Asia. In North America, this species winters on large lakes, rivers, and reservoirs, and along seacoasts across the United States and southern Canada. Common Mergansers nest primarily in tree cavities, but they will also nest on the ground or in crevices. Aside from small fish, they eat aquatic animals such as insects, mollusks, and worms, as well as frogs and some plants. Mergansers are sometimes known as "fish ducks," because of their feeding habits, and also as sawbills, because their slender bills are serrated for grasping prey. Breeding males have iridescent greenish-black heads and brilliant white necks and underparts. Females have gray bodies and rusty-brown heads with crests.

Common Mergansers are often silent. During courtship, males produce several calls: a faint, high-pitched, bell-like note; a twanging *uig-a*; and, during courtship flights, a call sounding like *kragagagagaga*. Calls given when males are alarmed or disturbed are hoarse *grrr*s and *wak*s. The female alarm call is a harsh *karr* or *gruk*, which can turn into a *gruk gruk gruk*, and they also utter a higher pitched, rapid *cro cro cro* when calling young from the nest.

KING EIDER

— *Somateria spectabilis* —

The dovelike cooing calls and *kwacks* of several males.

King Eiders are beautiful, ornately plumaged sea ducks that breed in remote areas of arctic North America—few bird species nest farther north than the King Eider. They nest in a variety of tundra habitats, but generally in vegetation in low marshy country, often adjacent to lakes or ponds or on small islands. There they consume vegetable matter and the larvae of aquatic insects and crustaceans. King Eiders winter primarily near the southern edge of sea ice off Alaska and eastern Canada, and, rarely, along the New England coast. While at sea, eiders mostly consume mollusks, crustaceans, other small sea creatures, and algae. Male King Eiders are quite distinctive in their breeding plumage, with reddish-orange bills, pale green cheeks, and light bluish-gray crowns and napes; females are mostly reddish brown.

The most common call of a male eider, given chiefly while sitting on the water, is a soft, dovelike cooing, variously described as *urrr-urrr-urrr, how-it-who-who, croo-croo-croooo, gug-gug-gugguggug-grooooooooooo,* or a wavering *hoooooo.* Males may also give threat calls in the presence of their mates that sound like *kwack.* As for females, during their migratory flights they often give a murmuring growl; other female vocalizations include croaks and grunts.

RUDDY DUCK

— Oxyura jamaicensis —

The belching display call of a male.

The Ruddy Duck is a small, stocky, stiff-tailed duck appreciated for the male's striking, bright sky-blue bill and highly entertaining bubbling display. In this courtship display, a male beats his bill against his neck, producing a tapping sound and forcing air out of the feathers, which causes bubbles to appear in the water. The display ends with the male uttering a low belching sound. Ruddy Ducks breed primarily in the prairie pothole region of North America and they are common winter residents of brackish and salty coastal habitats and large inland water bodies. They are mostly carnivorous, feeding extensively on insects and crustaceans. Male Ruddys have bright reddish-chestnut upper bodies, light bellies, and dark, fan-shaped tails often carried in an upright posture. Females are duller and browner.

Male and female Ruddy Ducks are silent most of the year. During courtship, aside from the belching that males produce as part of their bubbling displays, they make only an *aa-anh* call. Females have two principal vocalizations: a nasal *raanh* used to call young and to threaten others, and a high-pitched, pure-tone call uttered when they are chased by males. Females also hiss when threatened.

SNOW GOOSE

— Chen caerulescens —

((🐦))
014

Typical Snow Goose calls, or yelps, given by a migrant flock.

The Snow Goose is a medium-sized goose with plumage either mostly white with black wing tips or gray-brown with a white head. It is one of the most abundant species of waterfowl in the world, as well as one of the noisiest. It breeds in often-dense colonies north of the tree line along the coast and on islands in arctic and subarctic Canada. It winters in various parts of the contiguous forty-eight states and in northern Mexico. A voracious forager, the Snow Goose feeds on roots, aquatic and agricultural plants, and waste grain.

This goose's primary vocalization is a loud nasal *whouk, kowk,* or *kow-luk,* uttered by both sexes, at any hour and in any season, both in flight and when on the ground. Other sounds include feeding calls, a series of guttural *gah*s; alarm calls, penetrating *kaah-ahh*s; and flight calls—choruses of shrill falsetto cries, hoarse honks, and high-pitched quacks.

RUFOUS-BELLIED CHACHALACA

— Ortalis wagleri —

((🐦))
015

The raucous calls of chachalaca are a common morning sound in many parts of the tropical Americas.

Chachalacas and their close relatives, the guans and curassows, are chickenlike birds that live in tropical and sub-tropical regions of the western hemisphere. Perhaps the most attractive chachalaca species, the richly colored Rufous-bellied Chachalaca is confined to western Mexico. There it inhabits lowland deciduous and thorn forests and sometimes moves into agricultural areas, such as tree plantations. This bird usually appears in pairs or small groups, foraging in trees or on the ground for tree fruit, its staple food.

Chachalacas are perhaps best known for their loud morning and evening calls, which often sound like *cha-cha-LAW-ka*; a chorus of these calls is one of the most characteristic background sounds of many tropical forests in the Americas. The particular call of the Rufous-bellied sounds like *kirr-i-i-kr* or *chrr-uh-uh-rr*.

GOLDEN EAGLE

— Aquila chrysaetos —

One of the Golden Eagle's many subtly different calls.

One of North America's largest predatory birds, the Golden Eagle is dark brown with long, broad wings. It is widespread in the Northern Hemisphere, where it frequents a variety of habitats ranging from arctic to desert. Rare in the eastern half of North America, this species is relatively common and widespread in the West, dwelling in and around open spaces that provide hunting areas and often near cliffs that supply nesting sites. The Golden Eagle has astonishing speed and maneuverability for its size and uses several hunting techniques to capture prey, including soaring, still-hunting from a perch, and low, searching flight. These birds eat mainly hares and rabbits but also ground squirrels, prairie dogs, and marmots.

Golden Eagles are largely silent except during the breeding season, when up to nine distinct calls are recognized: *chirp, seeir, pssa, skonk, rattle-chirp* or *cluck, wonk, wip, honk,* and *hiss*. The most common are the *skonk* and *wonk* calls, which resemble yelping or mewing. The eagle produces *skonk*s in threatening or alarming situations, and *wonk*s as greetings when mates approach or meet each other. Males may emit long series of brief *wip* calls, interspersed with an occasional *wonk*, during food deliveries to young at the nest.

PEREGRINE FALCON

— *Falco peregrinus* —

((017))

The harsh nest-defense calls of a pair of Peregrine Falcons.

One of the world's most widely distributed birds, Peregrine Falcons range from tundra habitats to the tropics and from wetlands to deserts. In North America, these falcons breed from northern Alaska and Canada south to parts of Arizona and along the Atlantic coast. Peregrines are often considered symbols of wilderness, yet these strikingly beautiful birds now breed on many bridges and skyscrapers in the hearts of large cities. The name "peregrine" means "wanderer," and northern-nesting peregrines are among North America's long-distance migrants, some traveling up to 15,000 miles annually. Peregrines eat many species of birds, as well as some bats and rodents. They are famous for their stooping behavior, in which they dive from above at a very high speed to overtake and catch fleeing prey, usually in flight but occasionally as the prey runs on the ground or swims in water.

Peregrines are vocal mostly near their nesting areas. They give the chitter, a harsh *kak-kak-kak-kak*, often repeated incessantly, in alarm and in conjunction with nest defense. Falcons use the eechip, a sharp, deliberate *ku-ee-chip, ku-ee-chip,* in some courtship displays and during aerial encounters with other falcons. Finally, they use the wail call, a querulous *waiiiik*, in a variety of contexts, including the defense of self, territory, or food.

OCELLATED TURKEY

— Meleagris ocellata —

The courtship gobble of a male Ocellated Turkey, used to attract a mate.

The world's only two species of turkey are native solely to North America. The Wild Turkey, familiar to many, ranges widely over the United States and many other locales where people have transported it, such as Europe and Australia. But the lesser-known Ocellated Turkey lives only in Mexico's Yucatan Peninsula and adjacent parts of Guatemala and Belize. It inhabits low-elevation wet forests and clearings, as well as open brushy areas. These large, striking, ground-dwelling birds are an iridescent bluish black to blue-green, with bright blue, featherless heads that sport yellow-orange "warts." They usually spend their time in small groups, foraging for seeds, berries, nuts, and insects. The Ocellated's name comes from the eye-like images (*ocelli*) adorning the bird's plumage. Owing to overhunting and destruction of its forest habitats, the Ocellated Turkey is now at risk; it has been eradicated from some parts of its native range, yet is still hunted, even in nature preserves.

Ocellated Turkeys make a variety of sounds, including some similar to the well-known gobbling of Wild Turkeys and domestic turkeys. Observers note that when males are courting females, they emit a nasal *puhk-puhk-puhk-puhk* while displaying; females utter soft, clucking calls.

WILD TURKEY

— Meleagris gallopavo —

((019))

The familiar gobble of a male Wild Turkey.

The Wild Turkey, found only in North America, occurs from southern Canada south through the forty-eight contiguous states. A game bird noted for both its elusiveness and its delicious meat, it is now, thanks to modern game management, distributed over a wider range than it was prior to European settlement. Strong short-distance fliers, turkeys roost in trees at night but spend most daylight hours on the ground. They consume chiefly vegetable matter but also some insects and the odd salamander.

The male Wild Turkey's familiar *gobble* call appears to be closely related to the crowing-type calls of chickens. This call attracts females from a distance and repels competing males. Gobbling elicits gobbling from other males, so when one male of a group gobbles, others join in. Other major call types include alarm calls and various kinds of yelping sounds: the plain yelp, a general call given by both sexes; the tree yelp, given by both sexes before flying down to ground; and the "lost" yelp, given by both males and females as they attempt to reassemble after their flock has been scattered. Other calls are cackles, rattles, hisses, and coos.

WILLOW PTARMIGAN

— Lagopus lagopus —

((🐦))
020

Several calls given by a male Willow Ptarmigan trying to attract a mate.

The largest and most numerous of North America's three ptarmigan species, the Willow Ptarmigan is a bird characteristic of the arctic and subarctic tundras, breeding in Alaska and across a wide swath of Canada. These grouse are specially adapted for living in their extremely cold and snowy northern environments. They have feathered feet that function as snowshoes, they can use snow burrows for shelter, and they have all-white camouflaging plumage in winter. When breeding during the summer, females are brown and males are chestnut and white. They eat buds, twigs, leaves, insects, berries, and seeds.

Both ptarmigan sexes produce an array of calls. *Kok* is a short clucking call given between mates during foraging and also during territorial, sexual, and predator interactions; *ko-ko-ko*, a low growling utterance, may signal the intention to fly; they give a call that sounds like *bugow* in males and *meow* in females during aggressive disputes and as a contact call between mates or between parents and young; the *rattle*, an accelerating string of short notes similar to *kok*, is a territorial advertisement and defense call. Both sexes also make hissing and screaming sounds, usually during defense of nests or broods. Females make a *purr* sound, probably when alarmed.

CALIFORNIA QUAIL

— Callipepla californica —

The assembly call of a California Quail, rendered as *cu-CA-cow*.

The California Quail is native only to westernmost North America but, due to transport by humans, it is now also found in Hawaii, New Zealand, Australia, Germany, Chile, and Argentina. This attractive game bird, with its characteristic black head plumes and familiar call, is the state bird of California. It occupies scrubby habitats primarily in California, Oregon, and Washington, feeding on seeds, leaves, berries, insects, and flowers from grasses, shrubs, and trees. It lives in coveys, or flocks, that move within a certain range during the nonbreeding season. During the breeding season, the covey breaks up and individual pairs spread out to nest and raise their young. Males have boldly patterned black-and-white faces; females have brownish gray heads.

Both California Quail sexes produce the assembly call, a loud *cu-CA-cow*, usually uttered when an individual is separated from a group or a mate, and before and during covey movement. Quail contact calls consist of repeated notes, such as *ut-ut*, *mo-mo*, and *pit-pit*, which they give when they move as a group, when they discover food, and when they sight a predator. Only the males give the advertisement call, a single *cow* sound.

WHOOPING CRANE

— Grus americana —

((🐦))
022

The duet calls of a pair of Whooping Cranes.

The Whooping Crane, a national symbol of efforts to recover endangered species, has returned from the brink of extinction, increasing from only fifteen or sixteen individuals in 1941 to several hundred today. It remains one of the rarest birds in North America. The only self-sustaining wild population nests in Wood Buffalo National Park in the Northwest Territories of Canada and winters on the Texas coast of the Gulf of Mexico. A small population has also been established in central Florida. The tallest bird in North America, some whoopers reach nearly five feet. These birds take food from the ground, water, and vegetation, and they are particularly fond of snails, clams, crayfish and other crustaceans, insects, minnows, frogs, and snakes.

Whooping Cranes produce ten or more call types, but the common name of the species probably derives from its guard call or unison call. The guard call is a loud call associated with aggression or fear, given as an individual approaches or threatens other cranes. Males and females use the unison call in a coordinated duet; it functions in pairing and pair-bond maintenance.

VIRGINIA RAIL

— Rallus limicola —

((🐦))
023

The female's nocturnal *kicker* call.

The Virginia Rail is a secretive freshwater marsh bird that is more often heard than seen. A brief glimpse of its reddish bill and short, upturned tail is often all that observers see. This rail occupies a variety of wetland habitats, probing mudflats and shallow water with its long, slightly down-curved bill as it searches for snails, beetles, spiders, small fish, aquatic plants, and the occasional seed.

Virginia Rails' most frequent call is a grunt, given in duets by mated pairs. It functions in pair communication and territorial defense, often being produced during hostile interactions with other rails. Other calls are a *tick-it* sound, thought to function as a courtship signal by unpaired males holding a territory; and the *kicker* call, which probably functions as a breeding call when given by unpaired females.

AMERICAN COOT

— *Fulica americana* —

((🐦 024))

The *puhk* contact calls of a male.

One of the continent's most familiar wetland birds, the plump American Coot, with its black head and distinctive white bill, is the most aquatic, most abundant, and most widely distributed rail (a type of marsh bird) in North America. Coots consume aquatic plants, some terrestrial vegetation, mollusks, crustaceans, insects, and even some fish and tadpoles. They are raucous and quarrelsome birds whose presence is often announced by their loud cackling, grunting, and croaking calls given from deep within tall stands of aquatic vegetation.

Particular coot calls include those exchanged between members of breeding pairs, high, clear *puhk*s in males and low nasal *punk*s in females; territorial warning notes—in males a quick *puhk-ut, puhk-uhk, puhk-uk,* and in females a nasal *punk-unk, punk-uh, punk-unk-uh*; and alarm calls, *puhlk* in males and *poonk* in females.

AMERICAN AVOCET

— Recurvirostra americana —

((🐦 025))

A pair of alarmed American Avocets gives a series of repeated, melodic *kleek* notes.

American Avocets are large, striking shorebirds with long bluish legs and a long, thin, upturned bill. They are found in such wetland habitats as salt ponds, pothole lakes, the mudflats of inland lakes, water impoundments, and evaporation ponds. Avocets generally feed by wading in open shallow water, using their highly sensitive bill either to catch prey they see first or to probe into the water to snatch prey their bill touches. They consume insects, brine shrimp and fairy shrimp, worms, small fish, and the seeds of marsh and aquatic plants. Avocets breed in various inland wetlands of the western United States and Canada and along the coasts of parts of California and Texas.

American Avocets give several types of calls, which can be categorized as alarm calls, flight calls, and contact calls. All three types sound similar, but they differ, for instance, in pitch or rate of repetition. Avocets give alarm calls when they are highly agitated, such as when they dive-bomb potential predators. These calls, repeated *kleet* or *kleek* notes, can intensify to screaming sounds.

RUDDY TURNSTONE

— Arenaria interpres —

((🐦))
026

The chattering alarm call, given mainly by males.

The Ruddy Turnstone is one of the most northerly breeding species of shorebirds. In North America it nests in the northernmost tundra regions in Alaska and across arctic Canada, and it winters along the Atlantic, Pacific, and Gulf coasts. During breeding, Ruddy Turnstones eat mainly flies. However, during winter and while migrating they feed on rocky and sandy beaches, using their stout, strong, slightly upturned bills to dig or turn over rocks, pebbles, seaweeds, and shells in search of insects, crustaceans, mollusks, worms, and even small fish. Breeding individuals are boldly marked with black and orange, but winter adults and juveniles are colored with more subdued browns.

Ruddy Turnstones are highly vocal birds, often described as noisy, and males are more vocal than females. One of their primary calls is the contact rattle, a short staccato chuckling or twittering *kitititit*, given throughout the year, but mostly outside the breeding season as the birds flock together along the shore or in flight. Other calls include the alert call, a sharp, metallic *teuk* or *keu* given on the ground or in flight and used to warn other individuals; and the chattering-alarm call, given mainly during breeding, and described as a strong, metallic *TITwoooTIT-woooRITititititititititit*.

DUNLIN
— *Calidris alpina* —

((027))

An alarm call given on the breeding grounds.

The Dunlin, a small sandpiper, is among the world's most widespread shorebirds. It is a familiar species both in its striking summer breeding plumage, with a black belly and a reddish-brown back, and during winter, when it is gray and nondescript. They are found in flocks of thousands, and breed on subarctic and arctic coastal tundra from southwestern Alaska east to James Bay in Canada. During winter they occur mostly on large estuaries along the Pacific and Atlantic coasts of the United States. In some areas, such as the Central Valley of California, substantial numbers of Dunlin move inland from the coast in midwinter. Clams, worms, insects, and tiny crustaceans figure prominently in the diet of this species.

The Dunlin generally sings only in breeding areas, both on the ground and in air. This song, given primarily by males and infrequently by females, consists of a series of trills. It often begins with a *drurr-drurr* sound, followed by a falling-off, humming trill and ending with a subsiding *tri-ririri*. Others describe it as froglike wheezes, *wrrrrrah wrrrrrah wrrrrrah*, or as a twittering whinny, *chrri-i-i-i-i-i-ri-ri-ri-ri-ri-ri*. Males also give trill-like calls when flying.

WILSON'S SNIPE

— Gallinago delicata —

((🐦))
028

The winnow of a snipe, produced by the wings as the bird dives toward earth, is given during a display flight to attract a mate.

One of the most abundant and widespread shorebirds in North America, the Wilson's Snipe, formerly called the Common Snipe, breeds in bogs, swamps, and marshy wetlands throughout Canada and the northern United States. This bird is elusive; it is usually seen as it flushes from vegetation, escaping in rapid, zigzag flight while giving a hoarse, rasping note. During spring migration, and particularly on breeding territories, this species engages in spectacular flight displays, during which individuals produce a haunting, tremulous sound, known as winnowing, created by air flowing over their outstretched outer tail feathers.

A rasping *scaipe*, uttered when snipe are flushed, is the only vocalization given outside the breeding season. During breeding, several calls sounding like *jick, chipper,* and *geck GAEH,* are uttered in various situations including male-female interactions. Winnowing, a *hu-hu-hu* sound, serves as this species' territorial advertisement "song."

JAMAICAN LIZARD CUCKOO

— *Saurothera vetula* —

((029))

The long, drawn-out, rattling song of the elusive Jamaican Lizard Cuckoo.

Birdwatchers visiting Jamaica often search for the Jamaican Lizard Cuckoo, one of more than twenty-five bird species found only on that Caribbean island. In fact, the world's four species of lizard cuckoos—large Cuckoos that eat lizards—live only in the West Indies. The Jamaican Lizard Cuckoo occupies wet forests or woodlands. It forages by moving slowly through tree canopies in search of its wide range of animal foods, including many kinds of insects, lizards, and nestling birds.

Jamaican Lizard Cuckoos, because they tend to stay in tree foliage, are more likely to be heard than seen. They have a low, throaty voice, and their common vocalization is a rapid *cak-cak-cak-ka-ka-ka-k-k* that trails off at the end.

BLACK-LEGGED KITTIWAKE

— Rissa tridactyla —

((🐦 030))

The characteristic kittiwake calls, given at a nesting colony.

The Black-legged Kittiwake is widely distributed around the northern coasts of North America, where it is among the most sea-going of the continent's gulls. It winters far off the Atlantic and Pacific coasts. While breeding, it stays closer to shore, mainly in the arctic and subarctic regions of Canada and Alaska. Unlike most gulls, the Black-legged Kittiwake usually nests on vertical sea cliffs, laying its eggs on narrow ledges. Also in contrast to most gulls, kittiwakes do not frequent garbage dumps. They feed at sea, taking small fish and other small sea creatures, such as crabs.

Kittiwakes have a number of calls. Among the most common are greeting, choking, and alarm calls. During the greeting ceremony, males and females stand side by side or face one another in the nest and make kittiwake sounds: *a-eh-al-eh* or *hi-e-eh*. During choking displays, the bird's beak progressively opens wider while the bird utters *a-a-a* or *ae-ae-ae-ae* or *ei-ei-ei-ei*. Some alarm calls sound like *oh, oh, oh, oh*. When the birds leave their nests, they utter characteristic *vap vap vap* or *vapf vapf vapf* sounds as they fly away.

BONAPARTE'S GULL

— Larus philadelphia —

The buzzy alarm calls of a pair of Bonaparte's Gulls in flight.

The smallest common gull in North America, the Bonaparte's Gull is a familiar and often abundant migrant and winter visitor across much of the continent. It winters in large flocks in coastal areas, but breeds solitarily or in very loose colonies around ponds, bogs, bays, and fiords in the remote coniferous forests of Alaska and Canada. During migration and in winter, it frequents inland lakes and rivers, as well as coastal bays, estuaries, and inshore waters. The only gull that regularly nests in trees, it is unusually graceful and dovelike in appearance with a light, buoyant flight. These gulls have black heads in summer and black ear spots on mostly white heads during winter. They eat small fish and crustaceans, insects, snails, and marine worms.

Bonaparte's Gulls can be remarkably quiet while migrating or breeding, but they are usually noisy while foraging in flocks. Their main call is a buzzy, twangy, drawn-out *kaa-aa-aa-aa-aa* given by both sexes in a variety of situations. Their alarm calls are loud, brief *keh*s or *keh-keh*s. They use a vocalization known as their swoop-and-soar call, a very long *kreeeeeeeeee*, in aggressive situations such as when they dive toward intruders or predators.

MARBLED MURRELET

— *Brachyramphus marmoratus* —

Keer calls, from a pair of Marbled Murrelets flying through an old-growth forest nesting area.

The Marbled Murrelet is unique among members of its avian family, the group that includes puffins, in that this small seabird usually nests high in trees of coastal old-growth forests in Alaska and western Canada and along the West Coast. The species was once referred to as the "enigma of the Pacific" because of its secretive behavior and elusive nests. After more than a century of unsuccessful attempts to locate its nests in North America, the first verified specimens were found in 1974. Marbled Murrelets dive beneath the ocean's surface and pursue prey underwater. They eat small fish during the breeding season, and both fish and crustaceans the rest of the year. To feed their young, they fly at high speeds between feeding sites—protected coastal waters—and breeding sites in coastal forests, sometimes many miles inland. Breeding individuals are mostly brown, but wintering birds are black and white.

Marbled Murrelets emit three general vocalizations: Keer calls, which sound like *keer*, *kee-or*, or *kee-ee-er*, are most commonly given at nesting sites, while flying, and at sea. Their other two vocalizations are whistle calls, abrupt and forceful *kee*s or *eyaand*s, and groan calls, plaintive and whining, sounding like *eeh-eeh*.

MEXICAN PARROTLET

— Forpus cyanopygius —

((033))

The common contact call of the Mexican Parrotlet, a repeated *kreeit . . . kreeit.*

The Mexican Parrotlet belongs to a group of small, stocky, green parrots that can be very difficult to spot against a tree's green foliage, despite their vocal chattering. Often, this tiny green-and-blue parrot is clearly visible only in flight. The Mexican Parrotlet lives only in western Mexico in a variety of habitat types, including deciduous forests, dry scrublands, open grasslands with scattered trees, plantations, and woodlands along watercourses. It eats fruit such as figs, berries, and some seeds, which it finds in trees or on the ground. Mexican Parrotlets are highly social birds, typically convening in flocks of twenty to fifty or more individuals, although they are also sometimes found alone or in small groups.

These small parrots often call while perched in trees or flying. A common, far-carrying call sounds like a reedy *kreeit . . . kreeit* or *kree-eet . . . kree-eet*. They also give a variety of screechy, twittering vocalizations, which can make it sound as if there are more parrotlets in an area than are actually there. While feeding, they sometimes emit a solitary, squawk-like call.

ST. VINCENT AMAZON
— *Amazona guildingii* —

((🐦))
034

This loud *quaw . . . quaw . . . quaw* is a common call of this stunning parrot.

The St. Vincent Amazon is one of the most spectacularly colored parrots of the western hemisphere. This large bird is found only on the tiny island of St. Vincent, in the Lesser Antilles region of the West Indies, where it appears in two different colors: either primarily yellow and brown, or with an overall greenish hue. The species favors moist, mature forests, where it searches the tree canopy for its staple diet of fruit, seeds, and flowers. The St. Vincent Amazon is now rare and endangered. Its numbers started plunging in the early twentieth century, when developers cleared much of the birds' old-growth forest habitat for agriculture. The large, mature trees in which the St. Vincent Amazon nests were felled to make cooking charcoal. Furthermore, traders frequently captured these parrots for the illicit trade of exotic pets. By the mid-1980s, only about five hundred individuals remained; currently, with conservation efforts, probably more than eight hundred exist.

Although the St. Vincent Amazon has not been extensively studied, some of its vocalizations are known. Most observers report a loud call given in flight: *quaw . . . quaw . . . quaw* or *gua . . . gua . . . gua*. Other calls include a gutteral *screee-eee-ah*, a shrieking *scree-ree-lee-lee*, and, while feeding, drawn-out babbling or squeaking sounds.

PHEASANT CUCKOO

— Dromococcyx phasianellus —

((🐦))
035

A melancholy, whistled song of the rarely seen Pheasant Cuckoo rising from a Mexican forest.

This intriguing bird is one that few people see, even bird watchers seeking it. A species from the lowland regions of southern Mexico, the Pheasant Cuckoo is secretive and skulking, almost always sticking to dense undergrowth in the evergreen forests it prefers. It also occurs in Central and South America. Pheasant Cuckoos are fourteen to fifteen inches in length, with long, broad tails. They typically walk slowly and quietly through their wooded habitats, usually solitarily, foraging for insects (especially grasshoppers) and lizards. When alarmed, they run quickly from the source of disturbance, madly flapping their wings. The Pheasant Cuckoo is a brood parasite, which means that females lay their eggs in the nests of other species so the "host" birds raise their young.

Although people rarely see Pheasant Cuckoos, they often hear their calls. These birds, which spend most of the day on the ground, fly up to the middle or upper levels of trees to vocalize. Their usual call is a melancholy and far-carrying whistle: *se-see-werrrr* or *whee-whee-wheerrrr*. Another vocalization sounds like *sah*, *seh*, *si-see*, with the ending at a higher pitch than the beginning. These birds also make clucking calls.

YELLOW-BILLED CUCKOO

— Coccyzus americanus —

((🐦))
036

The *coo* call of a male yellow-billed Cuckoo.

Cuckoos are known worldwide for their bizarre habits, and the slender, long-tailed Yellow-billed Cuckoo is no exception. Furtive, retiring, and watchful by nature, this species' presence is often first revealed by its hollow calls. It has been dubbed the "raincrow" because of its apparent tendency to call more frequently on cloudy days. The breeding distribution of the Yellow-billed Cuckoo ranges mainly through the eastern two-thirds of the United States, although some breed in scattered western localities. They feed primarily on large insects—caterpillars, katydids, cicadas, grasshoppers, and crickets—but they also eat small frogs and lizards, and the eggs and young of birds.

The most frequently heard vocalization is the long, hollow, wooden-sounding kowlp call, rendered as *ka-ka-ka-ka-kow-kow-kow-kow-kowlp-kowlp-kowlp*. The kowlp, a male call, may be answered by another male and may function as a male-male "keep-away" signal; a male summoning his mate may also use it. Other vocalizations include the knocker call, a harsh, rattled, rapid series of notes, *kow-kow-kow-kow-kow*, that may coordinate feeding and nest-tending activities; and the coo call, *coo-coo-coo-coo-coo-coo-coo,* which may function as an advertising signal during pair formation.

SPOTTED OWL

— Strix occidentalis —

((037   ))

The male vocalization is a less common version of the territorial announcement song that contains five hooting notes rather than four.

The Spotted Owl is one of the most studied and best-known owls in the world. This degree of attention is the result of this bird's association with mature, old-growth conifer forests, which contain valuable wood. Commercial interests would like to cut down the trees in these habitats but environmentalists call for their preservation. The owl is an officially threatened species, and as such, under law, its habitat must be conserved—making the Spotted Owl highly controversial. These medium-sized owls are found primarily in California, Oregon, Washington, and British Columbia, but they also live in other scattered localities across the West. They nest in trees in forested areas and feed on rodents and other small animals, particularly flying squirrels and wood rats.

Spotted Owls communicate using a variety of hoots, barks, and whistles. Males and females typically use the most common call, a hoot sounding like *hoo-hoo-hoo-hooo,* to announce territorial occupancy and in territorial disputes. A hollow whistle *cooo-weep!* establishes and maintains contact between a pair, among other purposes. Barks described as *ow!-ow!-ow!-ow!-ow!* or *yenk!-yenk!-yenk!-yenk!* are used mostly by females during territorial disputes. The owls sometimes also produce a loud, grating *wraak!* when disputing territory.

PAURAQUE

— Nyctidromus albicollis —

((🐦))
038

Sounding like *p'weeEER*, the nocturnal song of the Pauraque is a common sound from southern Texas to Argentina.

A broadly distributed member of the nightjar family, the Pauraque ranges from northern Argentina northward through southern Texas, chiefly inhabiting forests and woodlands. It has a longish tail and appears in two different colors: either mostly greyish brown or reddish brown. Nightjars like the Pauraque are active at night and sometimes at dusk or dawn. They spend the daylight hours perched quietly either on the ground or on tree branches, where, because of their camouflage, they are almost impossible to spot. In parts of its range the Pauraque is known as *tapacaminos*, or "road-blocker," because of its habit of sitting on roadways at night and flying up only when people or vehicles get too close. Pauraques eat flying insects, which they hunt in the air, either by circling low over open areas or with repeated short flights from the ground.

Male Pauraques produce several different whistling songs, some loud and some soft. Those frequently uttered sound like *p'weeEER* and *whew whew whew whe-e-e-w*. Often these whistles are preceded by a string of *puk* or *put* notes: *put-put-put-put-p'weeEER*. Brief calls include *cluck* and *wup* sounds and also gutteral hissing. Females produce rapid *whip* calls.

AMETHYST-THROATED HUMMINGBIRD

— Lampornis amethystinus —

Like many hummingbirds, the Amethyst-throated Hummingbird
utters a variety of chips and buzzes while foraging.

The small Amethyst-throated Hummingbird is one of the prettiest of Mexico's more than sixty species of hummingbirds. It is a highland species, found in mountain forests at elevations up to almost ten thousand feet, zipping through the lower and middle levels of humid evergreen forests as it seeks flower-nectar nourishment. The species also lives in parts of Central America. The male's brilliant throat patch, or gorget, varies by region, from rose-pink to violet-purple. Females lack these colorful marks, and instead have throats of a dusky cinnamon color. Information on the ecology and behavior of this bird is limited, but researchers know that its cup-shaped nest is constructed from moss and lichens and secured to a small branch of a bush or tree. In addition to flower nectar, this hummingbird eats insects, which it chases and captures in the air.

Observers have described a number of different vocalizations for the Amethyst-throated Hummingbird. One that is given repeatedly, usually while the birds perch, sounds like a strong, chipping *chik chik chik . . .* , or *chiup chiup chiup . . .* , or *tsip tsip tsip . . .* While foraging they often utter a buzzy *tzzzzir* call.

RUFOUS HUMMINGBIRD

— *Selasphorus rufus* —

((🐦))
040

Chase calls, several sharp buzzes followed by three-syllable phrases.

The Rufous Hummingbird is North America's "extremist" hummingbird, widely known in the West for its aggressive nature. Venturing far from the equatorial tropics in which its ancestors evolved, this species breeds at the northernmost latitude of any hummingbird—as far north as southern Alaska, as well as south through the United States' Pacific Northwest. The species occasionally winters in the very southern part of California and along portions of the Gulf Coast, but mainly in Mexico. These birds feed on flower nectar and small insects and, when these foods are unavailable, tree sap. Males have a brilliant fire-red throat patch; the throats of females vary from whitish or streaked with bronze-green to having multiple red spots.

The vocalizations of Rufous Hummingbirds appear to serve mostly as aggressive threats, but they probably also have roles in mating. Both sexes give warning sounds, at feeders or on breeding territories, that sound like *chip, chip, chip*. If an intruding hummingbird passes over or refuses to leave, a territorial bird gives a rapid *eeeee didayer didayer didayer* or a raspy *eeech*. In flight, the wings of males emit a metallic whine.

RUFOUS SABREWING

— *Campylopterus rufus* —

((🐦))
041

The explosive *squihk* calls of a Rufous Sabrewing.

The Rufous Sabrewing is an attractive, medium-sized hummingbird with an especially broad tail. Resident only along the Pacific slope of southern Mexico and in small areas of Central America, it lives in rainforest habitats, some pine-oak forests, along forest edges, in canyons, and around plantations. Rufous Sabrewings hover at flowers to feed on nectar, and they capture insects in midair. When males discover particularly good nectar sources, they establish territories and defend the flowers from other hummingbirds.

Vocalizations of hummingbirds vary, but many species emit a number of short, high-pitched chirping or whistling calls and a brief, simple, quiet song. Calls of the Rufous Sabrewing include an explosive *squihk*, a metallic *pli-ik*, and a longer *chi-i-rr chik-chik-chik-chik*. Its songs range from chattering to warbling sounds.

AMAZON KINGFISHER

— Chloroceryle amazona —

((🐦 042))

The explosive rattling calls of an Amazon Kingfisher.

Handsome kingfishers occupy most parts of the globe, and in the Americas they are almost always associated with water. The Amazon Kingfisher, which is found from central Mexico to South America, is a beautiful dark-green representative of this group. In Mexico it lives along large rivers, lake shores, and in mangrove areas, and eats fish and crustaceans. To obtain food, this species observes quietly from a perch beside the water, then swoops and dives into the water to catch prey.

Amazon Kingfisher vocalizations include several loud, brief, harsh calls: *klek*, *chrit*, and *zzzzrt*. At times, some of these are rapidly repeated and strung together into a rattling sound. They also produce a series of clear notes that first rises and then falls in pitch.

CITREOLINE TROGON

— Trogon citreolus —

((🐦))
043

The trogon's territorial song from the mountains of western Mexico.

Wildlife lovers consider trogons to be among the world's most beautiful birds. They are found in the Americas, Africa, and southern Asia, but the Citreoline Trogon is uniquely Mexican, inhabiting the country's western slope in forests, woodlands, plantations, and mangroves. Trogons spend most of their time either singly or in pairs. Despite their brilliant colors, they are difficult to see as they sit motionless against green foliage on tree branches. More than most birds, trogons perch quietly for long periods, neither moving nor making sounds. The Citreoline Trogon eats fruit that it finds in trees, as well as insects plucked from tree leaves. Although these birds gather most food while they perch, observers have sometimes seen them taking tree fruit while hovering.

Generally, trogons possess simple, distinctive songs made up of various brief hootlike notes placed in different patterns and arrangements. Citreoline Trogons' songs consist of an accelerating series of *hoot*, *kyu*, or *cow* notes that become a chatter, described by one listener as sounding like *kyow-kyow-kyow-kyow-kyo-wkowkow*. The trogons sing all year, but their sounds are more frequent during breeding seasons. This species emits *kek* as an alarm call.

CUBAN TODY

— Todus multicolor —

((044))

The tiny and vocal Cuban Tody gives its rapid chattering *tot-tot-tot* call.

Todies are tiny forest and woodland birds that live only on the islands of Cuba, Jamaica, Hispaniola, and Puerto Rico. All five tody species look much alike, with bright emerald-green backs and heads, ruby-red throats, and whitish underparts tinged with yellow or pink. In fact, through most of the nineteenth century, they were all thought to be a single species. These little birds, related to kingfishers, are distinguished by their dazzling colors, their relative tameness, and their voracious feeding. Like hummingbirds, their tiny size means they have fast metabolisms, so they must feed frequently to replenish their energy. They eat insects caught in the air or pulled off leaves, as well as spiders, tiny lizards, and small fruits.

Todies vocalize often, sometimes almost continually, using brief, buzzy calls. The Cuban Tody is perhaps the most clear-voiced of the group, with a typical call that sounds like *pprreeee-pprreeee*. This vocalization may give rise to one of the local Cuban names for the species, *Pedorrera*. A common call, usually given while perched, is a rapidly chattering *tot-tot-tot-tot*. Another distinctive sound associated with todies is the loud whirring noise their wings make as they fly.

GOLDEN-CHEEKED WOODPECKER

— *Melanerpes chrysogenys* —

(((045)))

A common call of the Golden-cheeked Woodpecker is an explosive *ki-di-dik*.

The Golden-cheeked Woodpecker is a resident of western Mexico, where it inhabits forests, forest edges, open areas with scattered trees, and plantations. It is one of the region's handsomest woodpeckers, with its golden-yellow cheek and neck patches and black-and-white-barred back, wings, and tail. Only the male has a red crown; the female's is greyish. The ecology and behavior of this species are relatively unknown. It is usually spotted singly or in pairs, and is known to consume insects, including beetles and beetle larvae taken from trees, in addition to some seeds and fruit.

Many of the Golden-cheeked Woodpecker's calls are loud and nasal, especially a commonly given, explosive *ki-di-dik* call. A longer call sounds like *cheek-oo*, *cheek-oo*, *cheek-oo*, *keh-i-heh-ek*, and others contain "churring" sounds, like *churr-i-huh*.

BARRED ANTSHRIKE

— *Thamnophilus doliatus* —

((🐦))
046

The primary song of the Barred Antshrike from a tropical Mexican forest.

The Barred Antshrike, as its name implies, eats ants, but also many other kinds of insects. It is a small but striking representative of the antbird family, a large group of species restricted mainly to tropical areas of the Americas. The family is known especially for following swarms of menacing army ants in pursuit of the insects and other small animals that flee the advancing ants. However, the Barred Antshrike only occasionally forages by following ant swarms, often searching for food in ground thickets of the forest regions it inhabits from Brazil north to southern Mexico.

The song of the Barred Antshrike consists of an accelerating series of sharp nasal notes—*cow* or *cah*—that start out fairly soft but grow louder and conclude with a long, high-pitched, down-slurred note. Calls include growls, mews, and whistles.

- 92 -

IVORY-BILLED WOODPECKER

— Campephilus principalis —

((047))

The tapping and *kent* call of an Ivory-bill recorded in a Louisiana swamp in 1935.

Widely regarded as extinct, the Ivory-billed Woodpecker was reportedly rediscovered in 2005 in eastern Arkansas. The largest woodpeckers in the United States, they grow as long as twenty inches. Historically these striking, crested birds lived only in mature river forests and cypress swamps of the southeastern United States; however, development in the late-nineteenth and early-twentieth centuries significantly altered their habitat, causing the species' populations to plummet. Before their recent rediscovery, the last confirmed sightings of these birds were in the 1950s. Ivory-bills use their strong bills to strip bark from recently dead trees in search of their primary food, the larvae of large beetles. They also eat termites, fruit, nuts, and seeds.

The most distinctive vocalization of the Ivory-billed Woodpecker is its simple *kent* alarm call, given once or twice and often repeated. Observers have noted that another Ivory-billed call sounds like *pait*, *pait*, *pait*, or a high, rather nasal *yap*, *yap*, *yap*, both resonating like noises from a small tin horn. These woodpeckers also make surprisingly loud double raps by striking wood with their bills.

WHITE-STRIPED WOODCREEPER

— Lepidocolaptes leucogaster —

((🐦))
048

An example of the woodcreeper's long, territorial song.

Woodcreepers are small, slender, brown birds of the Americas. Like woodpeckers, they forage for insects by climbing quickly over tree trunks and branches, clinging to vertical and angled surfaces with the sharp, curved claws on their powerful feet and using their stiff tail feathers for support. Whereas woodpeckers attract attention with their "drumming" sounds and often bright color patches, woodcreepers are relatively quiet birds, usually drably dressed in brown, chestnut, and tan. The White-striped Woodcreeper is limited in its distribution to the highland forests and woodlands of western and southern Mexico. The species is usually encountered singly or in pairs, moving up tree trunks in search of insects hidden in bark crevices; they also join other kinds of birds in mixed-species feeding flocks.

Woodcreepers are known for their unadorned, unmelodic songs, most often consisting of simple rattles and trills. However, these songs are some of the most characteristic sounds of the forests in which these birds live. The song of the White-striped Woodcreeper sounds like a rapid, sputtering trill of twenty to thirty-five notes that slows at the end, like *zzzzzzzztztztztztztttt-t-t-bt-bt-bt*. A common call is also trill-like: *tsisirr* or *ssirrr*.

SCALED ANTPITTA

— Grallaria guatimalensis —

((🐦))
049

The hollow, rolling song of the elusive antpitta is often the only clue that it's in the area.

The Scaled Antpitta is a shy and retiring bird that occupies humid forests from central and southern Mexico south through parts of South America. A fairly uncommon bird that is rarely spotted, this species lives in the lower levels of the forest and on the forest floor, where it favors shady, dense vegetation, ravines, and areas near water. It forages by hopping about on the ground or on fallen trees, sometimes using its bill to turn over dead leaves as it searches for insects, worms, and millipedes.

The singing behavior of the Scaled Antpitta is not well documented, but its songs are known to consist of hollow-sounding notes that rise in volume and pitch over a four- to five-second duration. During breeding seasons, males sing from hidden perches up to thirty feet above the ground, and females may answer a male's song with a brief trilling vocalization. Scaled Antpitta alarm calls include croaking or grunting sounds. Because of this bird's stealthy demeanor, its songs and calls are usually the only evidence that local residents or visiting birdwatchers ever detect.

OLIVE-SIDED FLYCATCHER

— Contopus cooperi —

((🐦))
050

The male's song, *quick, THREE BEERS!*

With its favored prominent position, perched atop a large tree, and its characteristic resounding song, the Olive-sided Flycatcher is one of the most recognizable inhabitants of North America's coniferous forests. It breeds from sea level to 11,000 feet across Canada and throughout the western and northeastern regions of the United States, often in habitat along forest edges and openings. This flycatcher undergoes one of the longest migrations of all North American species, wintering primarily in Panama and the Andes mountains of South America. It feeds on flying insects, especially bees.

The Olive-sided Flycatcher's song—often described as *"quick, THREE BEERS!"*—is a distinctively loud and penetrating three-note whistle given primarily by males, presumably to attract mates and establish territorial boundaries. Both sexes give *pip, pip, pip* calls year-round, but especially during pairing, around the nest, and to keep in contact with mates.

HORNED LARK

— Eremophila alpestris —

A typical song given by a Horned Lark from the ground.

The Horned Lark is a widely distributed member of the lark family, and the group's only native representative in North America. It breeds over most of the United States, including Alaska, and much of Canada. With its signature but tiny black "horn" feathers, this lark occupies open, often barren, areas with very short vegetation, including agricultural fields. It forages on the ground, taking mostly seeds but also some insects.

Horned Larks sing in flight, when their song functions in courtship, or from a perch or the ground, when it may function in territorial defense. Some songs consist of about three notes rising in pitch followed by a rapid, slurred series of *chitter*s; others are long series of rambling notes, followed by rapid, slurred sounds. A commonly used call is a delicate *weet* or *su-weet*, which may function to maintain flock cohesiveness.

BLACK PHOEBE

— Sayornis nigricans —

(( 052))

The advertising song of a Black Phoebe, repeated *tee-hee* and *tee-hoos*.

North America's smallest black-and-white flycatcher, the Black Phoebe is a common species that breeds from California through the southwestern United States and Latin America. It is invariably associated with water because it needs mud to build its nest. Favored habitats are coastal cliffs, riverbanks, shorelines of lakes and ponds, and areas of parks with fountains. Black Phoebes eat mainly insects, which they usually capture by flying out from a low perch and snatching them in the air. They consume small prey in flight but carry larger insects back to the perch, where they are beaten and swallowed whole. Some phoebes capture small fish, and occasionally they eat berries.

Black Phoebe songs, used primarily for attracting females and in territorial advertisement, generally have two alternating sounds, described as *tee-hee* and *tee-hoo*. Some songs also contain *tieur* sounds, which are most commonly included when the birds are singing songs during mate association. A sharp *tsip* note, heard throughout the year and in several different contexts, is the most commonly given call. Other vocalizations are a chatter, a soft, wheezy sound males use when approaching females, and a *tweedle-deedle-eek* used during chases of mates and territorial intruders.

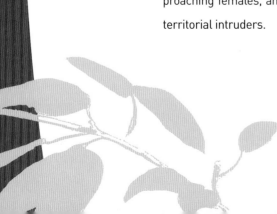

SCISSOR-TAILED FLYCATCHER

— *Tyrannus forficatus* —

((🐦))
053

The male Scissor-tailed Flycatcher uses its song in territorial defense and mate attraction.

Perched conspicuously on a wire or fence, its long tail trailing, the elegant Scissor-tailed Flycatcher is a common sight throughout the south-central United States during spring and summer. It favors open areas—savanna, grassland, shrubland, and agricultural and suburban habitats—with perches for feeding and trees and shrubs for nesting. It feeds by snatching insects from the air in graceful swoops and by perch-to-ground flights to take bugs from soil or low vegetation. Grasshoppers, crickets, and beetles are common foods. Individuals defend breeding territories and typically forage alone or in pairs. The species winters primarily in southern Mexico and Central America. The male's very long tail is, on average, three inches longer than his mate's.

Songs of male Scissor-tailed Flycatchers, sometimes given during flight displays, consist of repeated *pup* sounds followed by *perleep* or *peroo*. These songs are apparently associated with both territorial defense and mate attraction, and the birds sing them during early mornings and sometimes also at dusk. Other vocalizations, uttered by both sexes, include dry, harsh *pik, kip, bik,* or *kek* sounds, repeated *kee-kee* and *ka-leep* calls, slightly nasal *bik-errs*, and buzzy, chattering calls.

VERMILION FLYCATCHER
— *Pyrocephalus rubinus* —

((🐦))
054

The repeated territorial song of a male Vermilion Flycatcher.

Among the most spectacular of North American flycatchers, both in coloration and in courtship display, is the Vermilion Flycatcher, a common breeder in southern Arizona, New Mexico, and Texas. Males and females differ in coloring: the male's brilliant red crest and underparts contrast sharply with the whitish, lightly streaked breast and pinkish belly of the drab female. This species breeds in arid scrub areas, farmlands, desert, savanna, and woodlands, usually near water. During the breeding season, males perform remarkable flight song displays that reach sixty-five to one-hundred feet above the ground, during which they appear to bounce across the sky on fluttering wings while singing. These flycatchers forage from exposed perches, taking a variety of aerial and terrestrial insects, including butterflies, grasshoppers, beetles, and termites. They also eat spiders.

The male Vermilion Flycatcher's song, used in territorial formation and defense, courtship, and aggressive displays, is described as a repeated *ching-tink-a-le-tink!*, *p-p-pik-zee*, or *pit-a-zee*. The male's courtship flight song, given while flying a roughly circular path, is similar and has been described as a *t-t-ti-ti-tee-teeur* or *pt-pt-pre-ee-een*. This species' calls include brief chatters and sharp *peent* or *pisk* notes.

BLACK-BILLED MAGPIE
— *Pica hudsonia* —

((🐦))
055

An example from the Black-billed Magpie's wide repertoire of calls.

A common crow relative, the Black-billed Magpie mainly inhabits open areas of western North America, such as meadows, grasslands, and sagebrush deserts, but also occurs in river-associated thickets and some woodlands. These magpies, pretty and boldly marked birds, are typically seen in pairs or small groups, usually foraging on the ground or, rarely, in trees. They consume mostly insects, seeds, and carrion, but also small mammals, grain, and wild fruit; a major portion of their winter diet can consist of vegetable matter. They also eat other birds and their young, and in some regions are major threats to bird nests.

Black-billed Magpies have about fifteen different vocalizations. Only males produce one known as the soft song or whisper song of soft chatters and whistles, which may function as a territorial song. They also use a yelping call to proclaim territorial ownership. Most of the species' other vocalizations are brief calls. In general alarm and when attacking predators, they use often harsh and rattling calls known as *chatter*. They use a call sounding like *tchurch* during aggressive interactions and, in a softer voice, during courtship. *Squawk* and *shriek* are distress calls, given by both sexes when under attack.

BLACK-THROATED MAGPIE-JAY
— *Calocitta colliei* —

((🐦))
056

One of the many common calls from the Black-throated Magpie-Jay's wide repertoire of sounds.

One of the handsomest members of the globally distributed jay and crow family, the Black-throated Magpie-Jay inhabits woodlands and arid, brushy regions of northwestern Mexico. These jays, so striking that they are highly unlikely to be confused with any other bird in the areas they frequent, are usually spotted on shrubs or slowly flying between leafy trees. They have a black head and chest, a blue back, and a white belly; their extremely long tail, the longest of any of the world's jays, is deep blue edged with white. Black-throated Magpie-Jays usually associate in pairs or small groups, and feed on berries, fruits, insects, and spiders.

Jays are known for their often varied, piercing vocabulary, and the Black-throated Magpie-Jay is no exception. The species has a rich vocal repertoire, ranging from high-pitched and melodic to low-pitched guttural calls. Several calls are whistling notes, and others sound like yelps, clicks, or rattles. Often the jays rhythmically repeat a single call several times before uttering another. Some of the Black-throated Magpie-Jay's calls are described as a rolling *krrrrup*, a hollow, ringing *kyooh*, a raucous *krrowh*, and a nasal *rriihk*.

COMMON RAVEN

— Corvus corax —

((🐦))
057

The croaking calls of an alarmed raven.

The Common Raven, with its distinctly massive bill, is the world's largest songbird. In North America, it is found in Alaska, Canada, and the western and northeastern regions of the United States. It lives in a wide array of habitats, including forests and open environments, such as deserts, grasslands, and tundra, and now even in cities such as Los Angeles. The species prefers areas with cliffs that produce rising air currents, which yield favorable conditions for long-distance flight. Ravens generally hunt in flight or while walking on the ground. These large birds are often seen scavenging carrion—for instance, highway roadkill—but they consume a variety of foods, including rodents, nestling birds, fish, eggs, insects, grains, fruit, and garbage.

Common Ravens produce many kinds of sounds. Both sexes frequently give a loud call, known as a demonstrative call or a croak, to advertise their location and territorial ownership. Some of these croaks are long and undulating, while others sound like *rrock-rrock-rrock* or *calk-calk-calk-calk*. Female ravens utter knocking calls, which sound like woodpeckers hitting trees with their bills. Alarm calls include long, raspy, grating sounds and others that resemble a high-pitched *keck-keck-keck*.

VIOLET-GREEN SWALLOW

— Tachycineta thalassina —

((058))

Nighttime calls of the Violet-green Swallow.

The Violet-green Swallow is a common swallow of western North America, breeding from central Alaska southwards to the Rio Grande. It winters in Mexico and Central America. It occurs in an array of wooded habitats including higher-elevation coniferous forests and deciduous-coniferous woodlands. It often nests in inaccessible sites such as abandoned woodpecker holes in tall dead trees. Violet-green Swallows usually forage in small groups, flying high over the ground or low over fields or water. They eat only flying insects. Males and females look much alike; both are a striking metallic bronze-green above and have an iridescent violet rump, but females are duller.

These swallows have a limited vocal repertoire. Three vocalization types are *chee-chee, twitter*, and *zwrack* calls. The birds produce *chee-chee* calls when they associate with each other in many contexts—such as when individuals fly by each other, when traveling to and from nest sites, and during aggressive chasing. Twitter calls, uttered only in flight, are used during swallow interactions involving courtship and territory establishment. The *zwrack* call may be used as an alarm signal.

PURPLE MARTIN

— *Progne subis* —

((🐦))
059

A portion of a typical Purple Martin song.

The Purple Martin, the largest of North America's swallows, is unusual because in parts of its range, especially in eastern North America, it now nests almost exclusively in human-crafted birdhouses. As a result, these pretty birds are familiar to many. The species occurs mainly in the eastern half of the continent, but also in various regions of the West, where it breeds less frequently in association with people, preferring forests and woodlands and nesting in natural tree cavities or woodpecker holes. For food, martins pursue flying insects in the air, often flying higher than other swallows. Males are purplish blue overall, whereas females have dull gray underparts.

Purple Martins give about ten different vocalizations. The *croak* song, often containing grating or clicking sounds, is the males' primary courtship signal, given in the presence of females, and the *chortle* song is the females' courting vocalization. The species' loudest vocalization is its dawn song, given during early mornings, perhaps to attract other martins. They use a *hee-hee* call when fighting over territories. Females utter *choo* calls when signaling their fledged young. Two alarm calls sound like *zwrack* and *zweet*.

RED-BREASTED NUTHATCH

— Sitta canadensis —

The common, repeated *yank-yank* call of the Red-breasted Nuthatch.

The Red-breasted Nuthatch is a common forest bird of the United States and Canada. It is probably best recognized for the nuthatch habit of walking not just up tree trunks in search of insect food, but also *down* tree trunks, head first. The species occurs predominantly in coniferous forests but also in some mixed coniferous-deciduous woodlands. The Red-breasted Nuthatch's diet consists largely of insects and spiders, as well as conifer seeds outside of the breeding season. When foraging, these nuthatches use their bills to probe bark crevices for hiding bugs and to extract seeds from conifer cones; only occasionally do they forage on the ground. They excavate nest cavities in old dead trees.

Red-breasted Nuthatches give a range of calls throughout the year, particularly between mated individuals. Their most characteristic vocalization, a nasal *yank-yank*, probably serves multiple purposes. To attract females, unmated males on the breeding grounds give the courtship song, a plaintive, nasal *waa-aa-ns*. Another song, a harsh series of *hn-hn-hn* notes, is the most frequently heard vocalization of males during the breeding season, and probably functions as a territorial advertising song.

BROWN CREEPER

— Certhia americana —

The male Brown Creeper's song, *tsee-tuti-sedu-wee*.

The Brown Creeper, a small, inconspicuous brown-and-white bird that breeds and winters throughout most of the United States and in southern Canada, is the only member of the treecreeper family found in the Western Hemisphere. It is noted mainly for its characteristic foraging method—it flies to the bottom of a tree trunk, climbs rapidly upward in a spiral pattern around the trunk, foraging as it goes, then flies down to the bottom of a nearby tree and repeats the process. The creeper, as it climbs upward, uses its long, pointed tail as a brace against the tree's surface. Creepers inhabit coniferous and mixed coniferous-decidu-ous forests, feeding on insects, spiders, and small amounts of seeds and other vegetable matter.

The Brown Creeper's song and many of its calls include *tsee* sounds. The male song, given most often during territory establishment but continuing through the breeding season, is a thin, high-pitched *tsee-tuti-sedu-wee*. Both sexes produce several brief calls throughout the year, particularly during foraging. The birds often produce a sharp *tseet-tseet* and a bell-like *zi-i-i-it* in flight, and use *chee* calls during various courtship activities.

MARSH WREN

— Cistothorus palustris —

((062))

The male's territorial breeding song.

Much more often heard than seen, the Marsh Wren is a common inhabitant of cattail and bulrush marshes over broad swaths of the United States and Canada. The species is known especially for its reedy, complex singing, its polygamous breeding, in which one male mates with multiple females, and its habit of building more nests than it needs for nesting. These wrens forage at or near the water's surface, in nearby shrubs, or on cattail stalks, taking mainly insects and spiders.

Male Marsh Wrens usually sing for extended periods, especially during early morning. The loud, persistent songs play a role in mate attraction and territorial defense and are sometimes uttered up to twenty times a minute. They are often described as mechanical sounding and trill-like, such as *tek-k-jijijijijiji-jrr*. Each male may have two to forty or more song types, each slightly different. Males and females produce a variety of brief calls. In the East, during nest-building, males give nasal, buzzy calls. In the West, both sexes use *click* or *chuck* calls to keep in contact and possibly to signal alert. They utter trills—*turr turr turr*—when chased by other bird species and when humans approach their territory.

CACTUS WREN

— Campylorhynchus brunneicapillus —

The male Cactus Wren's song, *char-char-char-char*.

The Cactus Wren, the largest wren in the United States, is a common and characteristic bird of the country's southwestern arid scrub and cactus areas. Noted for its loud voice and for being among the first birds to vocalize at or before sunrise, scientists recognize the species for its adaptations to desert life. For instance, these wrens can go without drinking water, instead obtaining all their water needs from their food and from cactus juice. Cactus Wrens mainly eat insects and spiders but also small reptiles and amphibians, seeds, and cactus fruit. They construct large globular nests, mostly of twigs and grass, in cacti or other plants.

The male Cactus Wren's song, often given from a prominent perch within his territory, consists of rhythmic and at times raspy repetitions of single notes: *char-char-char-char* or *rar-rar-rar-rar*. Females occasionally give similar, quieter songs. Male song functions to attract females and probably to establish and defend territories. Males give *scri* calls as they fight and chase each other during territorial disputes. *Growl*s are recognition signals, produced by individuals when they encounter their mates. *Rrrack* or *rrreek* calls may be used to locate family members.

WINTER WREN

— Troglodytes troglodytes —

((🐦))
064

The bubbling song of a male Winter Wren.

The Winter Wren, known for its amazing vocal performances, breeds on four continents. In North America it breeds across much of Canada and the northern United States and winters in the Southeast and along the West Coast. Primarily a forest dweller, it prefers coniferous forests when breeding, and often nests and forages near water. Winter Wrens eat mostly insects and spiders, which they take from the ground, low foliage, and tree trunks.

Winter Wren singing is often considered to be at a pinnacle of complexity among songbirds. Males utter loud, vehement, continuous five- to ten-second songs consisting of clear notes, buzzes, and tinkling trills. These songs presumably have roles in territorial defense and mate attraction. Brief calls, often given in groups of two, vary by region, but some sound like *timp-timp*, *check-check*, *chat-chat*, or *jip-jip*.

BLACK-CAPPED GNATCATCHER

— *Polioptila nigriceps* —

((🐦))
065

Sounding like *reeihr*, this is one of the gnatcatcher's most commonly heard calls.

Gnatcatchers are active, agile forest and woodland birds that wave or twitch their tails as they flit about tree foliage, seeking insect prey. The birds' rapid movements and constant tail-waving may help flush bugs from their hiding places. There are fifteen species in the gnatcatcher family, which is found only in the Americas; the Black-capped Gnatcatcher is a typical representative and lives in northwestern Mexico. Very small, slender birds, gnatcatchers are mainly bluish gray, with long, narrow, black-and-white tails and usually some black on their heads. The Black-capped Gnatcatcher inhabits arid and semi-arid thorn forest and scrub areas at low and middle elevations, and often forages in dense vegetation.

The male Black-capped Gnatcatcher's brief song consists of scratchy, warbling sounds. The species also has many calls, including ones that resemble *reeihr*, *meiyhrr*, and chattering noises.

AMERICAN DIPPER

— Cinclus mexicanus —

((🐦))
066

A portion of the dipper's typical breeding song.

The American Dipper is a small, stocky songbird that lives along streams. It is quite unusual because it forages in the water and actually swims. The species is distributed from arctic Alaska south to parts of California and Arizona. The fast-moving, clear streams with rapids and waterfalls that dippers inhabit flow through forests, prairies, arid sagebrush zones, as well as urban areas—the surrounding habitat is extremely variable. Dippers feed on aquatic insects, small fish, and fish eggs. They forage almost entirely in streams, by walking, swimming, and diving. They will, for example, jump from a rock into the water and dive to the bottom, snatching whatever prey they discover but staying submerged for no more than fifteen seconds. The species' name refers to its habit of making repetitive up-and-down bobbing movements.

Both dipper sexes produce loud, piercing songs composed of jumbles of single notes, repeated notes, and trills. These songs play roles in mate attraction and territory establishment, among other functions. Calls include a loud, short, harsh sound, *jik*, given singly or repetitively, which is used for signaling between adults; *grawk*, a call given in aggressive contexts when two dippers are close together; and *weep*, uttered by females near nests.

GOLDEN-CROWNED KINGLET

— Regulus satrapa —

((🐦))
067

The territorial song, a series of high, thin *tsee* notes followed by a trill.

The Golden-crowned Kinglet is a tiny greenish songbird that breeds across parts of Canada and the western and northeastern United States and winters over much of the forty-eight states. It prefers coniferous forests, but also lives in deciduous forests, often near edges of clearings. It is a hardy species, capable of wintering in places such as Maine and Montana, where nighttime temperatures fall well below zero. They build cup-shaped nests, of twigs, grass, moss, and bark high in conifer trees. These birds feed on insects, spiders, and mites. Females have a yellow cap, but that of the male is yellow and orange.

Songs of Golden-crowned Kinglets, used to proclaim territories, are high-pitched, usually described as a series of *tsee* or *tsooo* sounds accelerating into a trill—*tsooo-tsooo-tsooo-tsooo-tsooo-tsooo-whip-lipalip!* or *tsee-tsee-tsee-tsee-teet-lee-tle,* followed by a trill. Other songs consist of long series of notes, each rising in pitch. Brief calls given by the kinglets, perhaps to stay in contact as they forage in dense tree canopies, consist of high, thin *tsee* sounds, often repeated: *tsee-tsee* or *ti-ti-ti.* A brief, buzzy alarm call sounds like *zeet.*

RED-LEGGED THRUSH

— Turdus plumbeus —

((🐦))
068

A portion of the territorial song of a Red-legged Thrush.

The Red-legged Thrush makes its home throughout much of the West Indies. An often secretive denizen of forests, woodlands, plantations, and gardens, it is more noticeable during its breeding season, when its singing and aggressive behavior make it stand out. In settled areas this thrush tends to forage along roadsides during morning hours for its diet of insects, spiders, snails, and small frogs, lizards, and snakes. The appearance of this attractive thrush differs a bit by locale—on some islands, these birds have a reddish-brown belly and black throat, but in other regions they lack these markings.

Songs of the Red-legged Thrush are melodious but somewhat monotonous: a repetitious *chirruit, chirruit eeyu biyuyu pert squeer squit seeer cheweap, screeet chirri*. Frequently uttered calls include *weecha-weecha-weecha* or *cha-cha-cha*. When alarmed, these birds utter a high-pitched *wiit-wiit* or *wet-wet* sound.

TOWNSEND'S SOLITAIRE
— *Myadestes townsendi* —

((🐦))
069

A portion of the elaborate song of the Townsend's Solitaire.

The Townsend's Solitaire is a drab, inconspicuous thrush of higher-elevation coniferous forests, often those of mountain slopes. It is perhaps most celebrated for its fine singing and habit of vocalizing from exposed treetops. It breeds in western North America, and mainly winters at lower elevations in the western United States. These solitaires eat insects and spiders, which they take in the air or off tree trunks or the ground, and also berries and small fruits. They nest on the ground, often below sheltering rocks or logs.

The elaborate song of the Townsend's Solitaire, used as both a territorial signal and a courtship communication, consists of clear warbled notes, frequently given in rapid series and often with abrupt changes in pitch. Brief calls include *tew* and *waa*, used during territorial behavior, and *kree*, given as an alarm call.

VARIED THRUSH

— Ixoreus naevius —

((🐦))
070

An example of a typical note given by a male in song.

The Varied Thrush is a brightly colored thrush about the size of an American Robin. The species breeds in dark, wet forest interiors from Alaska and western Canada through the northwestern United States; it winters along the West Coast. These thrushes forage primarily on the ground, picking up insects from the leaf litter and also, especially in winter, eating fruit, berries, seeds, nuts, and acorns. Males are mostly blue-gray and burnt orange; females are similar but duller over-all and browner above.

The penetrating, haunting territorial songs of male Varied Thrushes are one of the characteristic sounds of northwestern forests. Each song is a whistled, almost-pure tone, about two seconds long. An individual usually produces many songs in series, separated by five to twenty seconds. A male will sing this way for ten to fifteen minutes from a high tree perch before moving to another tree and repeat-ing the performance. Both males and females produce two calls, *vree* and *churrr*, in aggressive situations with other thrushes and other bird species. A brief *chect* note is probably used as an alarm call, as is a low *chuk chuk* sound females give at their nests when disturbed.

SAGE THRASHER

— Oreoscoptes montanus —

Some typical phrases from the variable flutelike song of a Sage Thrasher.

A shy, gray, streaked bird of arid areas of the western United States, the Sage Thrasher is known for its long, melodious songs and for being largely restricted during breeding to a single habitat type—sagebrush desert. The species breeds from the Southwest north to Washington state, and winters in the Southwest and Mexico. Sage Thrashers forage mainly on the ground for insects, spiders, seeds, and small fruits.

Sage Thrasher songs consist of a rolling series of loud, mellow, whistlelike or flutelike notes that can last for several minutes without pause. Males generally sing from the tops of sagebrush plants. Singing during the breeding season often begins forty-five minutes before sunrise and continues through most of the day; some individuals even sing at night. Males also sing during courtship displays, where they fly in circles over their sagebrush desert territories. Their songs probably function in mate attraction and territory maintenance. Like mockingbirds, these thrashers include the mimicked vocalizations of other bird species in their songs. Calls of Sage Thrashers include a *chuck*, given as an alarm call, and a whistlelike *wheurr* or *whee-er*.

EASTERN YELLOW WAGTAIL
— *Motacilla tschutschensis* —

The explosive *pseeu* call of a wagtail is given by both sexes, often while in flight.

From June through August, the Eastern Yellow Wagtail is a locally common breeding songbird in northern and western Alaska. On the Alaskan tundra it favors open shrubby and grassy moist areas, and it is conspicuous in these habitats with its bright yellow underparts, its characteristic wagging tail, and its persistent vocalizations. Wagtails feed on the ground, especially along the edges of rivers and ponds and in wet meadows, eating terrestrial and aquatic insects, spiders, and mollusks. Alaskan wagtails winter in eastern Asia, and the species also breeds in Asia.

Yellow Wagtails have two song types. Given from perches or during in-flight courtship displays, the courtship song sounds like a high-pitched *tzee-zee-zee* or *ter-zwee ter-zee zwee-zwee*. Territorial song, given from the ground or from perches around the perimeter of a male's territory, is a loud, sharp *tsee-wee-sirr tsee-wee-sirr*. The wagtails' most frequent calls, given by both sexes, are brief *pe-weet*, *pseeu*, or *tsit* sounds, which probably function in multiple ways, including maintaining contact when foraging and as alarm calls when predators approach nests. While hovering over a predator, the birds utter *kee* or *zeep* calls.

BOHEMIAN WAXWING

— Bombycilla garrulus —

((🐦))
073

The contact trills of a foraging flock of waxwings.

Bohemian Waxwings are intriguing songbirds that lack true songs. These gregarious, strikingly handsome birds breed in Alaska and northern Canada and winter in the northern United States and southern Canada. They are named for the red, waxlike tips they sport on some of their wing feathers, as well as for their nomadic wintering habits, when flocks travel widely seeking their preferred food—ripe fruit. They breed in coniferous forests, especially near water, but spend winters in a variety of habitats wherever fruit is available, usually parks and gardens. They eat primarily sugary fruits but also consume insects, plant buds, flowers, and tree sap. They sometimes act like flycatchers, flying out from fixed perches to snatch flying insects.

Most likely because the Bohemian Waxwing is not territorial—its main food, fruit, does not lend itself to easy defense—it has no territorial song, as most songbirds do. The most frequent calls of the species are trills and clear whistles. The basic trill, used for communication within flocks, is a high, hissing *zir-r-r-r*. They use other trills as courtship signals. They give brief whistles in an array of situations, including interactions between mates.

PHAINOPEPLA

— Phainopepla nitens —

The whistled *wheedle-ah* phrase, commonly given in male song.

A slender, crested bird with a long tail and red eyes, the Phainopepla is a characteristic species of the Sonoran and Mojave deserts of the southwestern United States. It occurs in arid woodlands and brushlands, including chaparral, mesquite, and Joshua tree habitats and around seasonally dry riverbeds. In brushy desert breeding areas, mated pairs nest alone and defend feeding territories against intruders, but at woodland breeding sites, Phainopeplas often nest in loose colonies made of three to fifteen pairs. These striking birds feed on fruits and small berries, particularly mistletoe berries, which they take from shrubs, and flying insects, which they catch by making short flights from perches. Males are glossy black and females are gray.

Songs of male Phainopeplas, which probably have a role in mate attraction, consist of a series of short sounds that typically include a whistled *wheedle-ah*. A very common brief call, often uttered while the birds flick their tails, is rendered as *wurp* or *hoi;* it may have several functions, including communicating alarm. The birds produce *churr* notes of two types—loud and harsh, possibly when they function in aggressive interactions, and soft, as both sexes use them during courtship. Phainopepla sometimes mimic the sounds of other bird species, such as hawks.

GREY SILKY-FLYCATCHER

— *Ptilogonys cinereus* —

075

Sounding like *chu-leep*, the common call of the Grey Silky-flycatcher.

A very handsome, slender bird with a bushy crest and long tail, the Grey Silky-flycatcher is one of only four species in the silky-flycatcher family. Members of this family live in North and Central America; the Grey Silky-flycatcher in particular occurs in highland areas over many regions of Mexico and in Guatemala. The group consists of medium-sized songbirds called silky-flycatchers, or "silkies," due to their soft and sleek feathers. These birds inhabit forests and woodlands, but also move about in more open areas with scattered trees. They feed chiefly by "flycatching"—they sit high on exposed perches, such as bare tree branches or tops of trees, and then dart out to capture flying insects. They also eat berries, particularly from mistletoe plants. Grey Silky-flycatchers typically keep company in pairs during breeding periods, but they form loose flocks, sometimes of more than a hundred birds, during other times of the year.

Silky-flycatchers are not considered strong singers, although two species in the family can imitate sounds of other birds. The song of the Grey Silky flycatcher consists of series of warbles and whistles usually produced at relatively low volume. Calls, often quite loud, include a nasal *chi-che-rup che-chep* and a sharp-sounding *chureet* or *chu-leep*.

RED WARBLER

— Ergaticus ruber —

((🐦 076))

The territorial song of a brilliant male Red Warbler.

One of the most striking and distinctive of the more than 110 species of American warblers is a bright red variety native only to mountainous regions of Mexico. Appropriately named the Red Warbler, this inhabitant of pine, pine-oak, and fir forests moves alone or in pairs through shrubs and the lower to middle parts of trees, in search of its main food, insects. Red Warbler pairs remain together all year, breeding at higher elevations and then moving to lower, warmer elevations for winter. They build nests of grasses, pine needles, and other plant materials on the ground amid dense vegetation.

Red Warbler songs consist of series of short trills mixed with rich warbles and occasionally high-pitched *chip*-like notes. Common calls include a strong *pseet* and a high, thin *tsii*.

KIRTLAND'S WARBLER

— Dendroica kirtlandii —

((🐦))
077

A typical Kirtland's Warbler song, from the Northern Michigan breeding grounds.

The rarest warbler in North America, Kirtland's Warbler breeds in a few counties in the central and northern regions of Michigan's lower peninsula and winters in the Caribbean. It nests only in stands of young jack pine trees. It was estimated that fewer than 200 breeding pairs remained in the 1970s and 1980s. Now, with conservation efforts, the total population is somewhere above 2,000. These warblers feed on insects taken from vegetation and the ground, and also small fruits.

Songs of male Kirtland's Warblers, which probably have both territorial defense and mate attraction functions, are loud, clear, and strident—a few low-pitched notes followed by a few higher, slurred ones: *chip-chip-che-way-o*. Other longer vocalizations, termed chatter songs, sound like *chu-chu-chu-chu*; while the Kirtland's common call is a high-pitched, faint *zeet*.

CHESTNUT-SIDED WARBLER

— Dendroica pensylvanica —

((🐦))
078

A male Chestnut-sided Warbler's mate-attraction song.

The Chestnut-sided Warbler is one of the most abundant warblers breeding in deciduous woodland and brushy thicket habitats of the northeastern United States and central and southeastern Canada. It also nests well in areas of regrowing woods around abandoned agricultural sites and timber-harvested clear-cuts. The species feeds chiefly on insects and also consumes some spiders, seeds, and fruit. Primary foods are caterpillars and other insect larvae, which these warblers seek by hopping around foliage and searching undersides of leaves. During breeding, Chestnut-sided Warblers are strongly territorial, defending the areas on which they feed and nest.

Male Chestnut-sided Warblers have two main songs. They use one, sometimes described as *please, please, pleased to meetcha* or *I wish, I wish, I wish to meet Miss Beecher*, as females arrive on the breeding grounds; it is thought to function in mate attraction. The other song, an aggressive, territorial song aimed at other males, is rendered as *wee-weewee-wee-chi-tee-wee*. Both males and females give various brief calls all year. Many are described as chipping calls, some sounding like *chidp*, others like *jrrt* and *zeet*.

MACGILLIVRAY'S WARBLER

— Oporornis tolmiei —

A male MacGillivray's Warbler song.

MacGillivray's Warbler is a generally shy and unobtrusive but common songbird that breeds from Western Canada through much of the western United States, especially in the Rocky Mountain region, and winters in Mexico and Central America. It inhabits dense brush and thickets at edges of coniferous or mixed deciduous-coniferous forests, often preferring wetter, sometimes river-associated, areas. The species eats insects taken on the ground or from low trees or shrubs, and nests on the ground. Males have darker heads than females.

Each male MacGillivray's Warbler has a single song type that contains six to eight phrases, as in *churry churry churry churry cheery cheery*. Each male's song is slightly different than those of other males, but all the songs are recognizable as emanating from this species. The bird sings to proclaim territorial ownership. Males sing another type of song while in flight. Both sexes of MacGillivray's Warbler utter brief calls. Males and females give a harsh *chip* when intruders approach their nests or young, and males also produce it during aggressive territorial encounters. Males and females also call out a high-pitched *chip,* perhaps as a warning to their young that danger is near.

OLIVE WARBLER

— Peucedramus taeniatus —

A male Olive Warbler's song, *peedo-peedo-peedo-peedo*.

The Olive Warbler is a small, fairly common songbird found only in a highly specialized habitat—mountain pine forests above 7,000 feet, from central Arizona to southwestern New Mexico. The species also occurs in Central America and Mexico. Birds of high tree canopies, Olive Warblers use pines almost exclusively for foraging and nesting. They feed mainly among high twigs and branches, only occasionally coming down to the ground to snatch prey dropped from higher up. Their diet consists primarily of insects. High on a tree's outermost branches, they build nests of moss, lichen, rootlets, pine needles, and other plant materials. Males have tawny-orange heads and upper chests; females are more yellowish.

Olive Warblers sing all year, but singing peaks during the spring breeding season. The songs consist of repeated whistled and buzzy notes; some contain only one kind of note, others contain two types. They have been described variously as *peedo-peedo-peedo-peedo*, *peter peter peter peter*, *tiddle-tiddle-tiddle-ter*, and *chroo-chroo-chroo-chroo-chroo-chroo*, and may function in territorial defense. Mated pairs give soft, whispered *phew* calls when foraging, perhaps to remain in contact.

WESTERN SPINDALIS

— Spindalis zena —

081

The high-pitched whistles of this species' song.

There are more than two hundred species of tanagers, which are petite, often gaily colored birds of North and South America, with reputations as fruit eaters. One small group of tanagers found only in the West Indies is called the spindalises. All four spindalis species, which in the past were known as striped-headed tanagers, look much alike. Males have a black-and-white-striped head and yellow under-parts, and females are more brownish or olive-colored overall. The Western Spindalis is a fairly common bird in the Bahamas, Grand Cayman Island, Cuba, and the Mexican island of Cozumel. It occupies a variety of habitats in these regions, includ-ing forest edges, woodlands, scrub, and shrub areas. In some places, the species favors pine trees during breeding. Usually seen in pairs or small groups, the West-ern Spindalis forages anywhere from low shrubs to high in trees, chiefly looking for berries.

Vocalizations of the Western Spindalis are numerous. Its songs, often sung from a high perch, include thin, high-pitched whistles described as *seet* and *deet* notes, sometimes accompanied by twittering sounds; another type of song consists of soft warbles. A frequently uttered call sounds like *seeip*, and a vocalization given in flight is *seet sit-t-t-t-t*.

WESTERN TANAGER

— Piranga ludoviciana —

((082))

An example of the raspy phrases delivered by a Western Tanager in song.

The Western Tanager male, outfitted in red, yellow, and black, is surely one of North America's most beautiful songbirds. The species is a characteristic bird of North America's western forests, and is the continent's—and, indeed, the world's—most northerly breeding tanager. It nests from Alaska's panhandle and western Canada south to the southwestern United States. Western Tanagers occur broadly within their range, inhabiting most open coniferous and mixed deciduous-coniferous forests and woodlands. They eat insects, taken from trees and shrubs, and also some fruit. Occasionally they act like flycatchers, snatching flying bugs from the air. The species winters in coastal southern California, Mexico, and Central America. Females are olive yellowish.

The Western Tanager song, given predominantly by males, consists of several strong, deliberate phrases: *pir-ri pir-ri pee-wi pir-ri pee-wi*. It is used to announce and defend territories. Both males and females possess several brief calls. They frequently produce a *pit-ick*, perhaps to give location information to each other as they forage in dense foliage. They make soft *wit* notes during courtship and other reproductive activities, and produce *pruree* calls when they are alarmed.

SCARLET TANAGER
— *Piranga olivacea* —

((🐦 083))

Several phrases typical of a male Scarlet Tanager's song.

A brilliantly colored songbird of high tree canopies, the Scarlet Tanager breeds across the eastern half of North America, from Maine and southeastern Canada south to northern Georgia. It winters in South America. It prefers deciduous and mixed deciduous-coniferous forests, but it also occurs in parks, orchards, and gardens with large shade trees. Males are bright red and black and females yellowish, but these birds, high above in leafy trees, are often difficult to see, especially given their somewhat secretive nature. Scarlet Tanagers feed on insects and spiders they capture on leaves, flowers, bark, and sometimes on the ground. They also dart after flying insects and take fruit from trees and shrubs.

Male Scarlet Tanagers sing from exposed perches in trees as soon as they arrive on their breeding territories in spring, often fairly constantly through the day. Their somewhat buzzy song is thought to function in territory establishment and defense, as well as in mate attraction and pair-bond maintenance. This song consists of four or five short, hoarse, nasal sounds, like *querit, queer, queery, querit, queer.* Some females sing shorter songs. Both sexes frequently utter *chip-churr* calls, especially when there are disturbances, such as potential predators, in or near their territories.

GREEN HONEYCREEPER

— Chlorophanes spiza —

((084))

The Green Honeycreeper alarm call, a sharp *tchiip*.

Honeycreepers are members of the tanager family, a large group of small, beautifully colored songbirds that are confined to North and South America. Tanagers have a reputation as fruit-eaters, but honeycreepers have specialized tongues and slightly down-curved bills that they use to probe flowers for nectar, sometimes by punching holes in the bottom of the blossom to drain it out. They also take small fruits, seeds, and some insect prey. Green Honeycreepers, which range from southern Mexico to parts of South America, usually frequent the high canopy of wet forests, but also come closer to the ground at forest edges, in clearings with scattered trees, and in gardens. They are typically alone or in pairs, often at flowering trees, where they occasionally hang upside down from leaves to reach particularly fine foods. Males are a brilliant, glistening green or blue-green with red eyes; females are yellowish green.

The vocal behavior of Green Honeycreepers is not well documented, but their song appears to consist of quiet buzzes followed by or mixed with trills or chitters, like *tst-tst-CHIT*, concluded with many *tst* sounds. One of their alarm calls is a sharp *tchiip*, and they give a *tssip* while flying.

BANANAQUIT

— Coereba flaveola —

((085))

The high-pitched trills and buzzes of the male Bananaquit's song.

An abundant bird of many Caribbean islands, southern Mexico, and much of South America, the tiny, yellow-breasted Bananaquit has a checkered history. At various times it was considered a kind of tanager or a warbler, but recent research suggests that it is not closely related to any other bird group, and therefore is the sole member of its own avian family. Bananaquits use their distinctive, slightly down-curved bill to search and pierce small flowers for nectar and to pierce fruits for juice. They also eat insects and spiders, and in some regions approach bird feeders that dispense fruit, especially bananas. The species, affectionately called *reinita* or "little queen" in parts of its range, lives in forests, wooded areas, gardens, and plantations, and in some areas visits outdoor restaurants to take sugar from tables.

Bananaquits sing during most of the year, and their vocalizations differ somewhat depending on the region, even among various Caribbean islands. In southeastern Mexico, the common song consists of a fast series of high, buzzy notes followed by a warbling trill: *tsee-tsee-tsee-tsee-tzzeew*. In other locations, the songs sound more like high-pitched trills, or buzzy, shrill twitters, or even short hissing sounds.

WHITE-CROWNED SPARROW

— Zonotrichia leucophrys —

((086))

A typical example of the male White-crowned Sparrow's advertising song.

One of the most studied songbirds of North America, the handsomely marked White-crowned Sparrow is a common breeder across Alaska, northern and western Canada, and in large sections of the western United States. For breeding, it occupies a variety of habitats: northern forests and tundra, alpine meadows, woodlands, grasslands, thickets, and roadsides. The requirements are dense shrubs or small trees where they can roost and place nests, and bare ground on which to forage. The species winters over much of the United States, inhabiting mainly brushy areas, including those in gardens and parks. White-crowned Sparrows eat insects, seeds, buds, grass, and fruit. Adults have black-and-white head stripes, whereas those of immature birds are brown and gray.

The advertising songs of male White-crowned Sparrows are sung year-round, but are more frequent during breeding seasons. Typical songs consist of one or more introductory pure-tone whistles, followed by buzzy notes and trills, sometimes described as *dear-dear-buzz buzz buzz*. Females occasionally also sing. The species produces about ten different, brief calls. *Pink*, given by both sexes, probably serves as an alarm signal, and the sparrows make a harsh-sounding *rasp* during aggressive interactions.

LAPLAND LONGSPUR

— Calcarius lapponicus —

((087))

An example of the male's advertising song.

The Lapland Longspur is a handsome, strong-flying sparrowlike bird that breeds in tundra habitats of Alaska and northern Canada. It is both one of the most common breeding birds in North America's high arctic and one of the most abundant wintering birds in the United States—mostly from the Great Lakes to Montana and south to Texas. The name "longspur" refers to the long claw on the hind toe of this and other longspur species. Lapland Longspurs feed on the ground, eating seeds and insects during breeding and seeds and parts of crop plants in winter. Winter flocks, some as large as four million individuals, occupy prairies and open fields, often settling in agricultural fields to feast on waste grain.

Male advertising songs in this species are rapid series of squeaky, jingling notes, variously described as *twee-twittle-uh-seetoo-twittle-uh-teeah-teeah*, *zing zizeleeaw zizelee-ee zizeleeaw*, and *churtle churtle seerilee-seerilee-serrilee seetle-we-we-you*. They sing these songs to maintain and defend territories and attract mates. The birds give brief calls, such as *chioo* and *kittyoo*, during foraging, most likely to stay in contact. Various alarm calls sound like *TEE-hu, dzeeu*, and *pitze-pitze*.

EVENING GROSBEAK

— Coccothraustes vespertinus —

The *cheer* and trill-like calls of a foraging flock of Evening Grosbeaks.

A plump, boldly colored songbird of northern forests, the Evening Grosbeak is a distinctive member of the finch family. It is a year-round resident across much of the western United States, the northern states, and parts of Canada. In some winters, however, when food is scarce, these birds move southward in flocks, searching for adequate food supplies, sometimes as far as central Texas. They breed in coniferous and mixed deciduous-coniferous forests and woodlands; in winter they can also be found in parks and at bird feeders. They eat insects and insect larvae, especially beetles and spruce budworm caterpillars, tree buds, fruits, and seeds, taking these items from tops and outer branches of trees and shrubs, and from the ground. Only males have yellow foreheads and eyebrows.

Evening Grosbeaks have three main vocalizations, none of which are much like the musical, complex songs of most other songbirds. The first is a frequently given flight call, a down-slurred whistle variously described as *cheer, peeer, p-teeee*, or *clee-ip*. The other two are trill-like calls and chatters. Evening Grosbeaks have another song, rarely used, which consists of a brief, rambling warble.

ROSE-BREASTED GROSBEAK

— Pheucticus ludovicianus —

The rich, warbling song of a male grosbeak.

The Rose-breasted Grosbeak, recognized for its bold colors and melodic vocalizations, is a relatively common songbird that breeds throughout much of eastern and central North America. It occupies several habitats, including woodlands and woodland edges, parks, and gardens, but it is especially partial to wooded areas along watercourses. Rose-breasted Grosbeaks occasionally take food from the ground, but their principal foraging sites are trees, usually at the periphery of leafy foliage. They eat insects, fruit, and seeds. Following their breeding, these birds migrate to Mexico and Central and South America for winter. Males are black and white with a rose-pink chest; females are brownish and streaked.

Both male and female Rose-breasted Grosbeaks sing. Their songs are considered similar to those of American Robins—rich, whistled, warbling sounds, often including one or more of the grosbeak's characteristic *chink* calls. Songs given by males function in territory establishment and maintenance, as well as in mate attraction and courtship. The distinctive, metallic *chink* is the most frequent call of these birds. *Squawk*, a harsh, loud, brief repeated call, probably serves as an alarm signal. Other calls sound like *chuk*, *weeur*, and *hrrr*.

NORTHERN CARDINAL

— Cardinalis cardinalis —

((🐦))
090

One male song variation of the Northern Cardinal, a ringing whistled *purty purty purty*.

The Northern Cardinal is a familiar, red-crested songbird found in the eastern half of the United States and in the extreme southwest. A year-round resident, it has developed a close association with people, breeding near their structures and taking food from their feeders. These pretty birds now also have small populations in California and Hawaii due to human transportation. Cardinals establish breeding territories in an array of habitats with shrubs and small trees, including forests, forest edges, woodland edges, marsh and stream edges, hedgerows around agricultural fields, parks, and suburban gardens. They forage on the ground and in shrubs and trees, consuming fruits, seeds, buds, and insects. Their bills are specialized to cut and crush shells to extract seeds. Males are a brilliant red, and females are brownish with a reddish tinge.

Both male and female cardinals sing. Songs are typically pure-toned, whistled sounds: *what cheer, cheer, cheer; cheer, cheer, what what what what;* or *purty purty purty*. Males sing during courtship and to defend their territories; females sing to communicate with mates and possibly to aggressively warn other females. The most frequently given calls of cardinals, which possess fifteen or more call types, are *chip*s, used in many situations.

DICKCISSEL

— Spiza americana —

((🐦))
091

An example of the Dickcissel's song.

The Dickcissel, a sparrowlike bird of the United States' central prairie region, requires a specific breeding habitat—open grassland with dense cover and tallish vegetation. Due to its semi-nomadic movements, its breeding abundance in any one area can vary dramatically from one year to the next. Dickcissels are also known for their polygamous mating habits, in which a single male mates with up to three or more females during a nesting season. They eat seeds during winter, and seeds, insects, and spiders when breeding.

Male Dickcissel songs usually consist of two introductory notes followed by five or six other notes, sounding like *see, see, dick, dick, ciss, ciss, ciss* or *see, see, quick, quick, sell, sell, sell*. A common, brief call of both sexes sounds like *chek* or *pwik*.

WESTERN MEADOWLARK

— Sturnella neglecta —

((🐦))
092

The familiar song of an advertising meadowlark.

The Western Meadowlark is an abundant, widely distributed bird of open, grassy habitats over much of the western half of North America. Not actually a lark, it is a member of the blackbird family. It is a characteristic inhabitant of grasslands, savanna, hayfields, orchards, pastures, and roadsides, and is familiar because of its loud, melodious songs. Meadowlarks feed on the ground, sometimes digging into soil with their bills. They eat weed and grain seeds as well as insects such as beetles, grasshoppers, and crickets.

Male Western Meadowlarks give their territorial songs from the ground or from exposed perches such as trees, utility poles and lines, and fence posts. Their songs, liquid and fluty, consist of several whsitled notes followed by a jumbled series of gurgling sounds, like *slip loo lidi lidijuvi*. A frequently uttered call is *chupp*.

ORANGE-BREASTED BUNTING

— Passerina leclancherii —

((093))

The Orange-breasted Bunting's warbling territorial song.

The pretty little Orange-breasted Bunting is limited in its distribution to arid areas of western Mexico, where it favors brushy woodlands, woodland edges, and thickly vegetated clearings. The bird is one of a group of seven colorful American species called buntings, which live mainly from southern Canada south to Central America, and which are closely related to birds known as saltators, cardinals, and grosbeaks. Orange-breasted Buntings, locally common in some areas, usually live in pairs or small groups. They typically search for food on or near the ground, taking seeds, fruits, flower buds, and some insects. Male and female Orange-breasted Buntings look much alike, although females are less blue and more green than males.

Songs of the American buntings are all somewhat similar, consisting of what are generally considered agreeable if sometimes overly persistent warblings, each lasting from two to five seconds. The Orange-breasted Bunting's warbling songs, usually given from a prominent perch, are a bit richer and sweeter-sounding than those of its closest relatives. Its most frequently heard brief call sounds like *tchik* or *chlik*.

RED-WINGED BLACKBIRD

— Agelaius phoeniceus —

((🐦 094))

The typical male song of a Red-winged Blackbird, *conk-a-ree*.

The Red-winged Blackbird, a marsh breeder, is one of North America's most abundant and most studied songbirds. It is known especially for its polygamous breeding system in which ten females may nest on the territory of a single male, and for its huge winter flocks, which sometimes cause significant agricultural harm. Red-winged Blackbirds breed in marshes, meadows, and croplands in parts of Alaska, across much of Canada, and through the entire lower forty-eight states. Some populations are migratory but others are year-round residents. They feed on the ground, on floating objects, and on vegetation, taking insects, seeds, and waste grain. Males, larger than females, are jet black with red shoulder patches; females are brown and streaked.

Male Red-winged Blackbirds each sing several versions of their familiar *conk-a-ree* or *o-ka-lee* song, each ending with a buzzy trill. These songs have roles in territory maintenance, as well as mate attraction and signaling. Females have two common songs, one a chittering sound, directed at their mates, and one a harsher buzzy sound, aggressively uttered at other females. Both males and females have an array of calls, *check* being the most common.

YELLOW-HEADED BLACKBIRD
— Xanthocephalus xanthocephalus —

A typical example of a male Yellow-headed Blackbird song.

Certainly one of North America's most strikingly marked songbirds, the Yellow-headed Blackbird is perhaps best known for its wetlands breeding habits and for it polygamous mating system—a male may have two to five or more females nesting in his territory. The species breeds from central Canada south to New Mexico, and from Indiana west to parts of California; it winters in the southern United States and Mexico. Yellow-headed Blackbirds nest in emergent vegetation, usually cattails or bulrushes, in marshes, lakes, and other wetlands, often with Red-winged Blackbirds nearby. They eat mainly insects during breeding seasons, and weed seeds and grain during winter. Males are larger than females, black with yellow heads; females are brownish with streaked bellies.

Male Yellow-headed Blackbirds produce two main songs, which distinctive but not very melodious. One, perhaps directed toward birds at distances, consists of several fluid notes often followed by a trill or buzz: *kuuk-ku, WHAAA-Kaaaa*. The other, directed toward closer birds, has a few clucking notes followed by a long, nasal buzz: *kuk-koh-koh-koh waaaaaaaa*. Females give harsh, nasal *cheee-cheee-cheee* vocalizations, which may be aimed at other females during aggressive interactions.

YELLOW-WINGED CACIQUE
— Cacicus melanicterus —

((🐦))
096

The cacique uses its song of various rattles and whistles to attract a mate.

The Yellow-winged Cacique is a striking black-and-yellow representative of the American blackbird family, which also includes such birds as grackles, meadowlarks, cowbirds, American orioles, and oropendolas. It stands out as one of the few members of the family with a noticeable crest. The species occupies lowland sites all along Mexico's western coast, and is found in habitats as diverse as forest edges, open areas with scattered trees, coastal scrub, and fruit plantations. These caciques are very conspicuous birds, usually spotted in the middle or upper parts of trees, in pairs or small flocks. They gather in the hundreds for night roosts, and breed alone or in small colonies of up to ten hanging nests placed near each other high in tall trees.

Yellow-winged Caciques are loud birds with a large repertoire of vocalizations. The species' song involves a rattling sound followed by quieter notes, described by one observer as *rrah, uh-uu, uh-uu, raahn'ee raahn'ee*. Calls include a number of whistles, rattles, harsh notes, and even ringing vocalizations like *ki-errr ink-ink-ink*. A very frequently uttered call sounds like *huik* or *whik*, and another is a nasal-sounding *raah* given with a rising pitch.

BOBOLINK

— Dolichonyx oryzivorus —

((097))

The complex, buzzy song of a male Bobolink.

The Bobolink is a handsome inhabitant of grassland environments, primarily across broad swaths of the northern United States and southern Canada. It is a long-distance migrant, wintering in the pampas grasslands of South America. The species historically bred in tall-grass prairies, but because these areas have been largely transformed for agricultural use, Bobolinks now often breed in dense hay-fields and weedy, wet meadows. Bobolinks are polygamous breeders, each male having up to three or more mates during a single nesting season. These birds forage on the ground or in low vegetation, eating insects and weed and grain seeds during breeding, and rice, oats, corn, and seeds during winter. Males—black, white, and tan—are sometimes described as wearing tuxedos backward; females are brown and streaked.

Male Bobolinks have a long, complex, bubbly song that sounds like *bob-o-link bob-o-link link wink bob-o-link*. Each male voices two song forms, one about seven seconds long and one about four seconds long. These songs function in territorial defense and mate attraction; the males often sing them while flying low over their territories in a characteristic fluttering flight. A frequently given call is *pink*.

RED CROSSBILL

— Loxia curvirostra —

An example of the Red Crossbill's variable song.

The lives of Red Crossbills revolve around conifer forests and conifer seeds, this bird's diet staple. Crossbills use their unusual crossed bills to extract conifer seeds—mainly spruce, pine, fir, and hemlock—from tough cones. The birds are fairly nomadic, wandering over large areas to find good crops of these seeds, stopping to breed only when a group finds a good supply. In North America, Red Crossbills breed regularly from southern Alaska and western and southern Canada south to Arizona and California. However, when wandering far and wide in search of seeds, these birds may breed as far from their usual haunts as Mississippi. Males are red, and females are yellowish green.

The songs of Red Crossbills consist of a few introductory notes followed by a warbled trill. Various listeners have rendered it as *pit-pit, tor-r-ree, tor-r-ree*; *whit-whit, zzzzt, zzzzt, zzzzt*; or *cheeree-cheeree-choop-chip-chip-chip-cheeree*. Females as well as males sing, but female songs are quieter and less frequent. Calls given in flight sound like *chip-chip-chip*. Birds in flocks give *chitter* calls, which may serve as communication within the flock. Alarm calls sound like *tut-tut* or *ooks-ook*.

COMMON REDPOLL

— Carduelis flammea —

((🐦))
099

The *che* calls of a winter flock of Common Redpolls.

The Common Redpoll is a lively, active, acrobatic little finch of arctic and sub-arctic regions. In North America it is a very abundant breeder in Alaska and northern Canada, wintering in central and southern Canada and the northern United States. A bird of far northern, open, coniferous forests and tundra scrub, the Common Redpoll spends much of its time flitting about trees and shrubs, often at the plants' outermost foliage, searching for small seeds. It also eats buds, some leaves, and algae, and sometimes forages on the ground. Specialized for life in cold northern regions, this redpoll has even been observed venturing into snow holes to feed on vegetation on the frozen ground. Only the male has a reddish chest.

The most frequent song of the Common Redpoll is comprised of repeated *che* or *cheh* calls, followed by or interspersed with *tschrrrr* trills: *che-che-che-tschrrrr, che-che-che-tschrrrr*, or *chuch-uch-uch-uch chuch-uch-uch-uch*. These songs may have both male-female and aggressive male-male functions. Brief *che* calls, often given incessantly while the birds forage, may help them keep in contact in dense foliage. Another common call is a nasal, drawn-out whistle, like *dsooee*.

PINE GROSBEAK

— Pinicola enucleator —

The whistled territorial song of a male Pine Grosbeak.

A large, stout finch, the Pine Grosbeak inhabits open coniferous forests from sub-arctic Alaska and northern Canada to Maine, as well as portions of the western United States. The species is most abundant near the treeline in far northern and mountainside forests, and near forest openings and edges, including near human settlements. It feeds in pairs during the breeding season and in flocks the rest of the year. Its primary diet consists of buds, seeds, and fruits, taken from trees, shrubs, or the ground, but these birds chiefly feed their young insects and spiders. They capture some flying insects in the air. Males are gray and rose-colored; females are gray and yellowish.

The songs of male Pine Grosbeaks, delivered loudly from perches near the tops of trees, consist of sequences of clear, fluty, whistling notes, rendered as *pee-lee-jeh pee-lee-ju*. These vocalizations have functions in courtship, pair-bond maintenance, and territorial defense. Long calls given in flight that might have roles in facilitating flock cohesion sound like *tee-tee-tew* or *pui pui pui*. While foraging in flocks, these grosbeaks utter quiet chittering sounds. An alarm call sounds like *chee-vli*.

SOUTH AMERICA

Known by some animal experts as the "bird continent," South America has more than three thousand bird species, many more than any other continent. This high number is due to South America's great variety of habitats, its many climates, and its complex landscapes, among other factors. Colombia and Peru, both much smaller than the enormous Brazil, each have over seventeen hundred bird species, more than any other country in the world; Brazil and tiny Ecuador each have about sixteen hundred species. The continent's other very large country, Argentina, has only about a thousand species, because, for the most part, it is not a tropical region, and bird species are usually most diverse in the tropics.

Some of the most celebrated birdwatching and other wildlife-observing locations in the world are in South America—the wonderful Amazon River region, the Pantanal wetlands of southern Brazil, and the magnificent Andes Mountains, which form the spine of the continent and run from Colombia to Chile.

A few of the birds for which South America is renowned are tinamous—primitive, ground-dwelling birds that are very weak fliers; screamers—large birds of wetlands that graze on aquatic vegetation; and potoos—owl-like birds that hunt nocturnally. Motmots—among the world's most beautiful birds with their brilliant greens and blues—and toucans, with their amazing cartoonish bills, are two other spectacular birds characteristic of this region. A final group that must be mentioned is the tanagers, an enormous assemblage of small fruit-eating bird species that come in all the colors of the rainbow.

UNDULATED TINAMOU

— Crypturellus undulatus —

((🐦))
101

The tinamou's whistled song is a familiar sound in South American forests.

Tinamous are highly camouflaged, usually secretive birds of South and Central America. Though chickenlike in appearance, they are related to larger, flightless birds such as the South American rheas and African ostrich. Tinamous can fly, but weakly, over short distances and usually close to the ground. Tinamous are difficult to study, but researchers have located the Undulated Tinamou in forest, savanna, and scrub habitats from Venezuela and Guyana southward to northern Argentina, an area that includes most of the Amazon region. Typical tinamou foods are fruits, seeds, and insects.

The loud, pure-toned, melodious whistles of tinamou songs are characteristic sounds of South American forests. Sometimes resembling notes from an organ or flute, these vocalizations often fill the forest all day long. In fact, the Undulated Tinamou makes one of the most common sounds heard in its tropical home— a melancholy call of three to four notes that rises in pitch at the end, like *doh doh doOH?*

CRESTED GUAN

— Penelope purpurascens —

((🐦))
102

The strident, piping call of a Crested Guan.

Guans are large, chickenlike birds that range over the warmer parts of the western hemisphere. The Crested Guan, an impressive bird almost three feet long, has a bushy crest, bare bluish skin around its eyes, and a red hanging throat sac. The species primarily inhabits wet forest areas from northern South America north to parts of Mexico. Associating alone, in pairs, or in small family groups, Crested Guans forage in trees for fruits such as figs and papaya, berries, seeds, and leaves, and they occasionally fly to the ground to take fallen fruit and beetles.

Crested Guans give incredibly loud honking and yelping calls, usually during the early morning and late in the day. Some sound like *kyeh-kyeh-kyeh* and *yoink-yoink-yoink*; others include a long, repeated *konh-konh-konh* and a guttural *kweeohh*.

HARPY EAGLE

— Harpia harpyja —

((🐦))
103

A loud *weeee-eww* is the common call of the Harpy Eagle.

A massive eagle that has long been considered the world's most powerful bird of prey, the Harpy Eagle is essentially the "top bird" from southern Mexico to northern Argentina. It grows almost three feet long from bill to tail tip and has a wingspan of six-and-a-half feet. Harpy Eagles stay mainly within vast tracts of remote, lowland tropical forest. They prey on a wide range of fairly large animals, especially monkeys and sloths, but also anteaters, raccoonlike mammals called coatis, opossums, porcupines, young deer, large parrots, curassows, and reptiles such as iguanas and snakes. In inhabited regions, these huge birds capture chickens, dogs, lambs, pigs, and small goats. They rapidly kill their prey, then take it to a treetop to consume it.

The Harpy's usual vocalization is a loud, strident scream, *weeee-eww* or *whee . . . whee . . . wheeu*. They also produce soft clucks and croaks.

SUNBITTERN

— Eurypyga helias —

((🐦))
104

The far-carrying call of the Sunbittern sounds like *eeeeeeeeeeeeeuree*.

Sunbitterns are about eighteen inches long and have beautifully patterned grey, brown, and black plumage, a black head with white stripes, a long, straight bill, a slender neck, and a long tail. They live along tropical, forested streams and around flooded forests, where they walk in search of insects, spiders, crabs, frogs, crayfish, and small fish. They are known for their spectacular courtship and threat display in which they spread their tails and wings to reveal a striking "sunburst" pattern of yellow, brown, and black. Sunbitterns are elegant but wary birds, usually appearing solitarily. They make rounded cuplike nests of leaves and mud that they place in trees or bushes. The species ranges from Guatemala southward to Peru and central Brazil.

Many of the Sunbittern's vocalizations are loud and far-carrying. In the early morning, it often gives a clear, high-pitched whistle that sounds like *eeeeeeeeeeeeeuree*. A striking, loud *kak kak kak kak* sound may serve as an advertisement call. It also sometimes emits a series of shorter calls, many of them whistled or trill-like, that rise or fall in pitch. When Sunbitterns are disturbed or alarmed, they produce a hissing *churr* sound.

GREY-WINGED TRUMPETER
— Psophia crepitans —

((🐦))
105

Loud, staccato calls typical of the Grey-winged Trumpeter.

Trumpeters, large birds with long legs and a hump-backed appearance, are terrestrial animals that inhabit dense tropical forests. One of only three trumpeter species, the Grey-winged Trumpeter is limited to parts of northern South America. In areas where trumpeters are hunted, they are very shy, and so are rarely seen. They feed by patrolling the forest floor, looking for fallen fruits and scratching with their feet to stir up insects. Their time in the air is generally limited to flights into trees to escape danger and to roost at night. Trumpeters almost always live in flocks of five to twenty or more. In some areas, local residents capture trumpeters to keep them as pets.

Generally, trumpeters are highly vocal birds. The calls they are named for are apparently used as territorial signals, although they do not always resemble trumpet sounds. Their namesake calls are often given at night, starting about two hours after sunset. The calls begin with three to five loud staccato notes quickly followed by a long note that descends in pitch, like *oh-oh-oh-oh-oooooooh*. Trumpeters also make various softer humming and growling calls, and often a *woop* call as they walk along the ground.

HYACINTH MACAW

— Anodorhynchus hyacinthinus —

((🐦))
106

Kraaa-aaa calls given by a group of foraging macaws.

One of the highlights of any birdwatcher's trip to Brazil's Amazon or Pantanal regions is discovering a flock of enormous, violet-blue Hyacinth Macaws, feeding, loafing, and squawking in a large fruit tree. Macaws are the largest parrots, and the Hyacinth, at about three feet long, is the longest of all macaws. The Hyacinth Macaw is completely blue, except for bare yellow skin around its eyes and bill and some black under its wings and tail. These birds associate in pairs or in small groups, often in palm groves or tall trees near rivers. They nest in cavities high in palms and other large trees, as well as in cliff-side cavities in some regions. These magnificent birds forage for food on the ground or in trees, eating palm and other fruits and some snails. After decades of exploitation for the illegal-pet trade, Hyacinths are now rare and classified as endangered.

The quite vocal Hyacinth Macaw emits a number of harsh or shrill calls. Their most common sounds are bursts of *kraaa-aaa kraaa-aaa* and *kraa-ee kraa-ee*, and their alarm calls are grating shrieks. When flying long distances, mated pairs usually fly high, keeping close and calling out to each other almost continually.

HOATZIN

— *Opisthocomus hoazin* —

(((🐦)))
107

A typical call of the noisy Hoatzin is a repeated *gaah-gaah-gaah*.

The Hoatzin, which lives only in northern South America, is one of the continent's most intriguing animals. A turkey-sized bird marked by a prominent crest and bluish face, it lives in the wet forests and marshes of the upper Amazon region. It is unlike any other bird species—some claim it looks like a small, feathered dinosaur. These strange birds usually flock in groups of two to eight and stay in bushes or small trees along the edges of slow-moving streams or forested lakes. They eat leaves only and have a digestive system similar to a cow's that uses fermentation to break down otherwise indigestible plant parts.

Hoatzins are noisy birds, and when members of a group start vocalizing together they cause quite a racket. They have a number of different calls; a common one is a low, hoarse *gaah-gaah-gaah-gaah*.

PAVONINE QUETZAL

— Pharomachrus pavoninus —

((🐦))
108

An emphatic *chok!* note, followed by a whistled call, *heeeeear*.

The medium-sized, compact-bodied birds known as trogons are widely considered some of the world's most visually stunning birds. Among the most beautiful trogons are the quetzals, and bird fanciers generally regard one quetzal, Central America's long-tailed Resplendent Quetzal, as the most spectacular bird of the Americas. The Pavonine Quetzal, with its shorter tail but similar red and emerald-green plumage, is a close runner-up. It lives in many portions of South America's Amazon region, usually remaining in the interior parts of humid lowland forests. Its food seems to consist mainly of fruit and insects.

The most frequently heard vocalization of the Pavonine Quetzal is a sequence of five notes, *ew ewwo-ewwo-ewwo-ewwo*. Another call is a loud whistle that descends in pitch, like *heeeeeear*, often followed by an abrupt *chok!* note.

GREAT POTOO

— Nyctibius grandis —

((🐦 109))

The nocturnal cry, *groaaaa*, of a Great Potoo.

Potoos are highly unusual looking and somewhat owl-like, due to their large heads, huge eyes, and upright posture. They are medium-sized, forest-dwelling birds that range from Mexico south into Argentina. The Great Potoo is the largest of the seven potoo species, living anywhere from extreme southern Mexico to southern Brazil. During the day, potoos sit in trees; with their camouflage coloring and their bills pointed skyward, they strongly resemble dead branches, making them very difficult for birdwatchers and others to spot. At night, potoos become active and hunt as solitary seekers of large insects and small birds and lizards. Their typical hunting strategy is to sit on a perch and make short flights out to catch flying insects. Potoos do not build nests; females lay a single egg in a crevice on a stump or large branch, often high in a tree.

Because they are rarely seen, potoos are mainly recognized by their mournful cries. The Great Potoo's most frequent call is a very loud, harsh-sounding *groaaaa* or *kwaaahw*, repeated about every ten seconds, mainly at dusk and on moonlit nights. Other calls include barking sounds and *grooks* upon being disturbed.

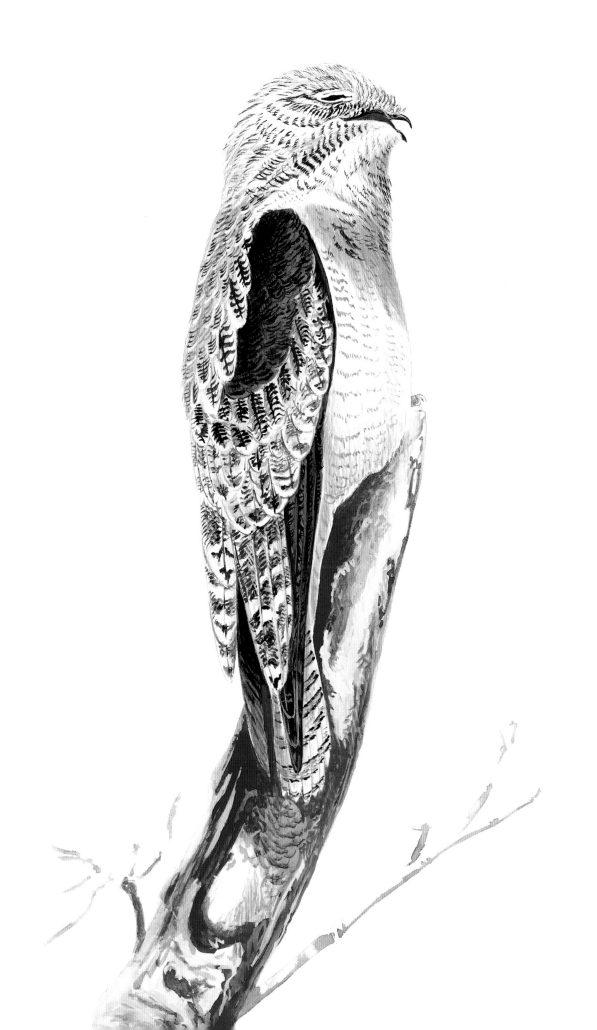

SWALLOW-TAILED HUMMINGBIRD

— Eupetomena macroura —

((110))

Several loud *tsak* notes from a perched Swallow-tailed Hummingbird.

The Swallow-tailed Hummingbird is among South America's most beautiful and unmistakable hummingbirds, with its deeply forked tail and brilliant green and violet-blue coloring. This species occurs in the Guianas, Brazil, and parts of Peru and Bolivia. Despite being somewhat common in many regions, these birds are not always easy to see because they do much of their feeding in the middle and upper parts of tall trees. They live in a variety of natural habitats, including forests, forest edges, and open, savannalike areas, but also in plantations, parks, and gardens. Swallow-tailed Hummingbirds feed on flower nectar, both from the trees they visit and from epiphytes, or "air plants," that grow on the trees' branches. They also catch insects in the air. This particular hummingbird species has a reputation for being highly aggressive, and actively defends good food resources from other hummingbirds by chasing intruders away from choice flowers.

Some hummingbirds have melodic songs, but most species, like the Swallow-tailed Hummingbird, have short, simple vocalizations. This hummingbird produces weak, twittering sounds, often interspersed with a *cha-cha-cha*. It also makes a loud *tsak* call.

RUFOUS MOTMOT

— Baryphthengus martii —

((111))

The territorial vocalization of the Rufous Motmot is a repeated, owl-like *hoop*.

With their striking cinnamon-and-green coloring, crisp black masks, and long tails with tennis racket–shaped tips, motmots are perennial candidates for the title of Latin America's loveliest birds. Birdwatchers who travel to the motmots' realm, from Mexico to central South America, always have these birds on their viewing wish lists. The Rufous Motmot, among the largest of the motmots at up to eighteen inches long, ranges from Honduras southward to northern Bolivia. These beautiful birds, residents primarily of tall, humid woodlands, usually live singly or in pairs, but do appear in small groups more often than other motmot species. They are versatile feeders, pulling fruits from trees while flying, and, at ground level, catching insects, spiders, crabs, small frogs, and lizards. They occasionally consume dangerous poison-dart frogs and capture small fish in water.

Rufous Motmots usually vocalize in the early morning, often from high up in the tree canopy. Their calls consist mainly of various series of owl-like notes: *hoop hoop huhuhuhuhu* or *ho-hoo-hoo* or *hoot hoot hoot*. Briefer calls sound like *HOOtoo* or *hoorro*. When agitated, these birds emit harsh chattering sounds.

COLLARED ARACARI

— Pteroglossus torquatus —

((🐦))
112

A piercing *pseeet* is the contact call of a foraging Collared Aracari.

The aracaris are a group of about twelve species of toucans known for being especially colorful, with brightly marked bills and long tails. All have underparts of yellow, red, black, or some combination of these colors. They range from Mexico to Paraguay, occupying mainly forested lowland regions. The Collared Aracari, which appears in Colombia, Venezuela, and northward into Central America, is one of the better-known members of this striking group. It inhabits wet forests and forest edges, and is usually found in pairs or small, noisy parties of five to fifteen individuals. Observers usually find these aracaris foraging or playing in tree canopies, hopping among branches or following each other in single file from one tree to the next. They eat fruits such as figs, papayas, guavas, and palm fruits—which they sometimes acquire by raiding tree plantations—as well as insects, lizards, and bird eggs and nestlings.

The most characteristic vocalization of the Collared Aracari is a high-pitched, piercing *pseeet* or *tseeep* note, often repeated in a rapid, staccato fashion. They also frequently emit a variety of rattles, chatters, and some purring calls. In aggressive situations they use an *arghrr* call; an alarm call sounds like *pit*.

BOAT-BILLED FLYCATCHER

— *Megarynchus pitangua* —

((🐦))
113

Loud, chattering vocalizations of a foraging Boat-billed Flycatcher.

One of a set of very similar-looking flycatcher species native to South America, the Boat-billed Flycatcher is recognized by its massive, broad bill. This striking bird is never abundant over its wide range, which extends from Mexico to southern Brazil, but it is nonetheless frequently spotted by birdwatchers who seek it. Boat-bills hunt from perches, scanning for prey, typically large insects such as cicadas, and then suddenly flying out to snatch the prey, often from foliage. These birds mainly live in pairs or small groups in wooded habitats, seeming to prefer semi-open areas such as forest edges and clearings with scattered trees.

The various vocalizations of Boat-billed Flycatchers are unarguably loud and grating. Typical gruff calls include a rattling *keerrrrr-eek*, a nasal *eehr*, *eehr ki-di-rrik*, and one that sounds like *quee-zika quee-zika*.

STREAMER-TAILED TYRANT

— *Gubernetes yetapa* —

((114))

The *tewear-TEE-tear* song, given during a courtship display.

One of the most spectacular flycatchers of central South America is the pale grey Streamer-tailed Tyrant. It prefers to live near water, frequenting marshes, streams, and wet grasslands. It perches on bushes or low trees, from where it makes repeated flights to chase and catch insects in the air, often swooping low over water or marsh vegetation. Both males and females have long, deeply forked tails, although female tails are slightly shorter. The species ranges from Bolivia and southern Brazil to northern Argentina.

Streamer-tailed Tyrants have an amazing courtship display, during which one sex perches above the other, flaps its wings, and excitedly utters whistled notes—*tewear-TEE-tear*—a few times; the mate responds with a warbled *tea-whittle, tea-whittle*. Calls include a loud, harsh *whee-irt!*, *weert!*, or *shrewip!*, sometimes repeated, and a down-slurred *ju-ju-ju*.

POMPADOUR COTINGA

— *Xipholena punicea* —

((🐦))
115

Male and female cotinga give a loud *purp* call.

A few species of cotingas, which are fruit-eating forest birds, are among the flashiest animals of South and Central America; the Pompadour Cotinga is undeniably a part of this rare group. Males are a shiny purple or crimson-purple with bright white wings, which make these birds immediately visible against the green tree canopies of their Amazon rainforest habitat. Females are much less showy than the males, being mostly sooty grey. The species favors dense forest canopies and some woodlands, where it feeds on fruits, primarily from various palm and fig tree species, as well as some insects.

The vocalizations of Pompadour Cotingas have not been thoroughly studied, but males are known to give a loud, croaking, mechanical rattle, and some observers report shrieking sounds as well. Both sexes utter a loud *purp* call.

GUIANAN COCK-OF-THE-ROCK
— *Rupicola rupicola* —

((🐦))
116

Several male Guianan Cocks-of-the-rock calling at an Amazonian lek.

Male Guianan Cocks-of-the-rock, deep orange with large, bushy crests, are one of the South American rainforest's brightest avian stars. These stunning, medium-sized birds gather near rocky outcroppings in groups of three to fifty or more to await females looking for mates. The birds typically use the same group-display sites, called "leks," for many years, even decades. The dark-brown females enter leks, decide which courting males to mate with, and then leave to nest on their own. Guianan Cocks-of-the-rock live only in northern South America and eat fruit and insects.

During aggressive displays aimed at rival males in leks, males utter loud calls, including one that sounds like a forceful *ka-krrow!* While foraging, Guianan Cocks-of-the-rock are often heard making a distinctive *waa-oww* sound.

PLUSH-CRESTED JAY

— *Cyanocorax chrysops* —

((🐦))
117

One of the common calls given by this vocal species.

The Plush-crested Jay is a conspicuous, slender-looking forest jay that ranges from central Brazil to northern Argentina. Its appearance is distinct: Its colors of violet-blue, black, and creamy white are striking, and its unusual crown of stiff, plush feathers forms a "cushion" on its head. Furthermore, it usually associates in noticeable groups of up to ten or twelve individuals that forage together, making quite a racket. The birds vocalize often and loudly as they move actively through trees, hopping from high to low as they search for food on leaves and branches; occasionally their search leads them to the ground. They eat a variety of things, including insects, spiders, fruits, berries, and the eggs and nestlings of small birds. These handsome jays sometimes visit orchards, plantations, land other agricultural areas, and are bold enough to take table scraps around settlements.

Like many jays, the Plush-crested Jay produces a wide array of loud, unmusical calls. The most frequent call sounds like *cho-cho-cho*. Other common calls are a ringing *iyok-iyok-iyok*, a metallic *kuh-kuhkuh*, and various croaks and gargles. These birds are good mimics, copying the vocalizations of other birds, and even those of local mammals such as monkeys.

BLACK-CAPPED DONACOBIUS
— *Donacobius atricapilla* —

((🐦))
118

The singing duet of a pair of Black-capped Donacobius.

The Black-capped Donacobius was long considered a mystery bird because biologists couldn't definitely determine what kind of bird it was. Because of its size, long tail, strong legs, and outgoing personality, it was thought to be a type of mockingbird. Now, after careful study, most believe this unique species is a type of wren, though this may not be the last word on the subject. Sleek and boldly marked in black, chocolate-brown, and buff, this songbird lives in most of northern and central South America. They inhabit marshy vegetation and grassy areas near lakes and slow-moving rivers, and are usually seen perched atop tall grasses, in pairs or small family groups. They feed on insects and other small invertebrate animals.

Loud and vocal, Donacobius are recognized for their duets, in which pairs perch near each other on marsh grasses, bobbing their heads and wagging their tails. One bird gives *chrrr* notes while the other chimes in with *kweea* sounds. Their calls include a loud *quoit-quoit-quoit* or *who-it who-it who-it* and a harsh *jeeeyaa*.

PARADISE TANAGER
— *Tangara chilensis* —

((🐦))
119

Typical calls of the brilliant Paradise Tanager.

Though it has the scientific name *chilensis*, the small, multicolored Paradise Tanager lives from Colombia and Venezuela southward to Brazil and northern Bolivia, excluding Chile. It is a bird of Amazonian forests, and often remains hidden in mid- to high-level tree canopies. Bird fanciers recognize it for its brilliant yellow-green head, its stiffened, scale-like head feathers, and its color variation: In some regions the bird's lower back and rump are an intense red, but in other areas its rump is bright yellow-orange. Paradise Tanagers move through the tree canopy, searching for fruits and insects, usually in groups of five to ten individuals in mixed-species feeding flocks with other tanager species.

The Paradise Tanager frequently gives a high-pitched, whistle-like call, *sizit* or *tsilip*, that it often repeats in a rapid series with *chip* notes, like *tsilip chip chip*. Its song seems to consist of combinations of *chak* and *zeee* notes, like *chak zeee*, *chak zee-a-zee* or *zeee-chak-chak-chak*.

OLIVE OROPENDOLA

— Psarocolius yuracares —

((120))

The explosive, gurgling display song of a male Olive Oropendola.

Birdwatchers visiting South America's Amazon region almost invariably see oropendolas. They are easy to spot as they fly between treetops because they are large, strikingly marked, and usually in small flocks. The Olive Oropendola, at up to twenty inches long, is one of the largest oropendolas, and one of the most beautiful, with its olive-green and chestnut body, pink bare-skin face patch, and yellow tail. The species usually appears in the high tree canopy of forests and forest edges, where it forages for insects, other small animals, and perhaps some fruits. It ranges from Colombia and Venezuela southward to central Brazil. Olive Oropendolas breed in small colonies of up to ten to fifteen pairs, and their long, hanging, basketlike nests, common to oropendolas, are a characteristic addition to high branches of tall trees in the areas in which they live.

During courtship displays, male Olive Oropendolas give loud, gurgling songs that begin with crackling or grating sounds and often end whiplike—*cc-rr-rr-rr-rr-whh-heeeeeoooooppp, tek-tek-ek-ek-ek-ek-oo-guhloop!* or *psooEE-OH, o, o, o, o, o, o, o*. Their most frequent call sounds like *chak*, and they frequently utter a *dwot* in flight.

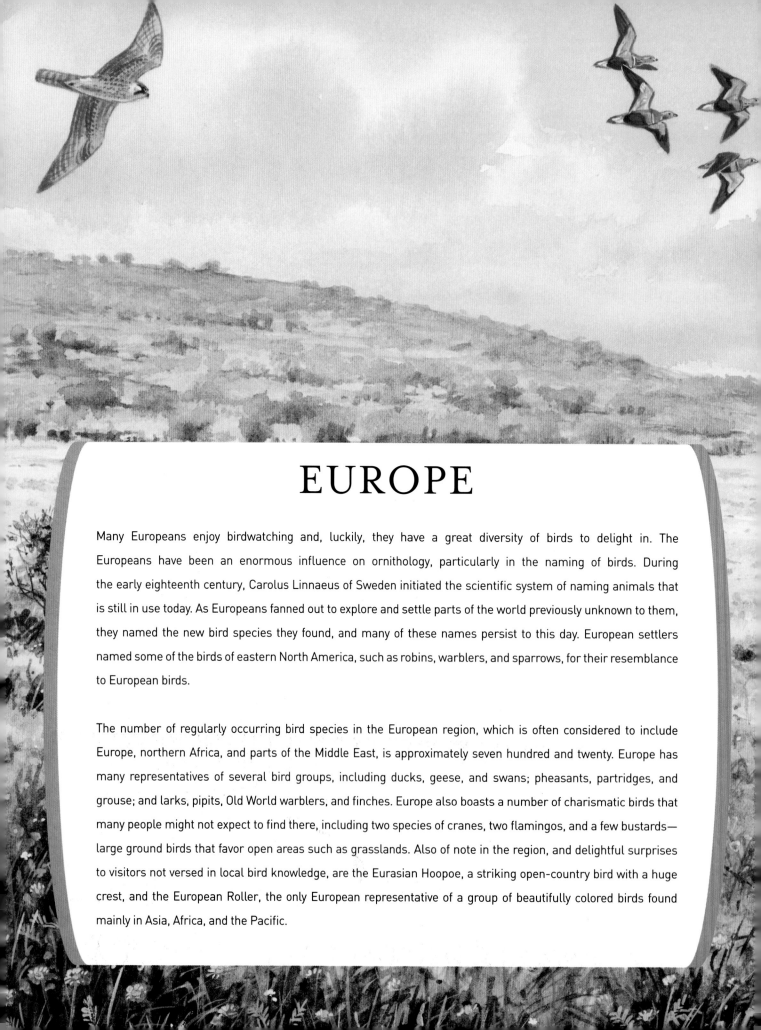

EUROPE

Many Europeans enjoy birdwatching and, luckily, they have a great diversity of birds to delight in. The Europeans have been an enormous influence on ornithology, particularly in the naming of birds. During the early eighteenth century, Carolus Linnaeus of Sweden initiated the scientific system of naming animals that is still in use today. As Europeans fanned out to explore and settle parts of the world previously unknown to them, they named the new bird species they found, and many of these names persist to this day. European settlers named some of the birds of eastern North America, such as robins, warblers, and sparrows, for their resemblance to European birds.

The number of regularly occurring bird species in the European region, which is often considered to include Europe, northern Africa, and parts of the Middle East, is approximately seven hundred and twenty. Europe has many representatives of several bird groups, including ducks, geese, and swans; pheasants, partridges, and grouse; and larks, pipits, Old World warblers, and finches. Europe also boasts a number of charismatic birds that many people might not expect to find there, including two species of cranes, two flamingos, and a few bustards—large ground birds that favor open areas such as grasslands. Also of note in the region, and delightful surprises to visitors not versed in local bird knowledge, are the Eurasian Hoopoe, a striking open-country bird with a huge crest, and the European Roller, the only European representative of a group of beautifully colored birds found mainly in Asia, Africa, and the Pacific.

GREATER FLAMINGO

— Phoenicopterus roseus —

Nasal calls given by a group of Greater Flamingos in flight.

Nature lovers immediately recognize flamingos by their upright stance and distinctive pink coloring. The Greater Flamingo, the largest of the world's five species, inhabits many regions, including southern Spain and southern France, where it is usually called, simply, "Flamingo." These stately birds, up to four-and-a-half feet tall, usually spend their time in salty ocean lagoons or alkaline inland lakes. Flamingos are famous for their "filter feeding": With their heads upside-down under the water and their bills resting on the bottom, they suck in water and mud, push it through comblike bill filters, and consume the tiny invertebrate organisms that they strain out. Greater Flamingos also eat mollusks, crustaceans, insects, worms, and even some seeds and decaying leaves. They are highly social, feeding and breeding in large groups.

Greater Flamingos are noisy birds, frequently uttering loud, gooselike calls. These sounds vary between high-volume cackles, trumpetlike notes, and deep grunts or growls. Some of these vocalizations are thought to play roles in keeping flocks together. When a flock is feeding, the birds emit soft, low "gabbling" sounds; in flight, they produce nasal honks.

BEAN GOOSE

— Anser fabalis —

((🐦))
122

The familiar honking vocalizations of a Bean Goose.

The Bean Goose is a scarce winter visitor to parts of central and northern continental Europe. During the winter, these birds gather in flocks of varying sizes and inhabit open-country sites such as marshes and agricultural lands, where they feed on leftover crops, including beans, corn, and potatoes. The species breeds at arctic and subarctic latitudes in Scandinavia and northern Asia, usually around lakes, rivers, or marshes. During breeding, they eat wild grasses, herbs, and berries. Like other geese, the Bean Goose is monogamous and seems to mate for life.

Vocal expression is a very important part of geese's social behavior, but the utterances of this particular goose are not well known. It produces a variety of calls, the most frequent sounding like a loud, nasal *ung-unk* or *yak-ak-ak*.

WESTERN CAPERCAILLIE

— Tetrao urogallus —

123

A male capercaillie displaying in the Scottish Highlands.

The Western Capercaillie is the largest and perhaps most striking member of the grouse family, which consists of medium and large-sized game birds restricted to the northern hemisphere. The species ranges from western Europe eastward to parts of Siberia, but is now scarce in many regions due to the destruction and alteration of its forest and woodland habitats, as well as overhunting. In Europe it is now most abundant in Scandinavia and in mountainous areas south of this region. Fortunately, conservation efforts have reintroduced the Western Capercaillie to areas from which it was formerly eliminated, such as Scotland. These grouse eat pine needles, leaves, and plant buds in winter and berries, sedges, and mosses in summer.

At dawn, male Western Capercaillie give long calls with clicking, popping, and hissing sounds. In the evening, when they gather into groups, males utter bellowing *ko-KRERK-korohr* calls.

LITTLE BUSTARD

— Tetrax tetrax —

((🐦))
124

The male Little Bustard uses this rattling call during its breeding display.

Bustards are large, long-necked, long-legged birds that are usually considered game birds. Most bustards live in Asia and Africa, but two species, including the relatively small, pheasant-sized Little Bustard, occur in Europe. Found in Spain, France, and parts of Italy, Little Bustards inhabit flat, open, grassy areas, as well as agricultural lands such as pastures and crop fields. Gregarious during non-breeding periods, these curious birds often keep to small groups, foraging for both plant materials, such as leaves, shoots, seeds, and flowers, and small in-vertebrates such as insects. Male Little Bustards have bold black-and-white neck patches when breeding, but females and nonbreeding males do not.

Rather quiet animals, Little Bustards vocalize primarily when breeding. The most common call accompanies the male courtship display, during which they stamp their feet on the ground, sometimes make a short jump into the air, and utter a soft, snortlike *prrt* every few seconds. Both on the ground and in flight, males also produce a whistling *sisisisisi* sound when they beat their wings. Females utter cackling or chuckling calls when disturbed.

DEMOISELLE CRANE

— Anthropoides virgo —

((125))

The raspy staccato calls of a pair of alarmed Demoiselle Cranes.

Most Europeans are aware of the charismatic Eurasian Crane, also known as the Common Crane, which breeds over many parts of the continent. But few recognize that another crane species, the Demoiselle Crane, also lives in Europe. However, it breeds there fairly rarely, and only appears in the extreme southeast, around the Black Sea. This mainly grey and black bird is the smallest of the world's fifteen cranes, but still quite large at about three feet tall with a five- to six-foot wingspan. Demoiselle Cranes favor savanna-like habitats and grasslands, usually remaining within easy flying distance of streams, lakes, or other wetlands and sometimes moving into agricultural districts. They forage on the ground for grass seeds and other seeds, worms, large insects like beetles, and lizards. At their wintering grounds in Africa, India, and China, they are quite social, and sometimes roost in flocks of thousands.

Calls of Demoiselle Cranes are usually low-pitched and raspy. When given in flight, particularly during migration, some of these vocalizations sound like *grro grro*. While these cranes are feeding, or when they meet other cranes, they emit low *purr*-like sounds. Alarm calls consist of brief bursts of raspy, staccato calls.

LANNER FALCON

— Falco biarmicus —

The shrill, piercing cry of a Lanner Falcon.

The large, beautiful Lanner Falcon is a rare bird in Europe. Perhaps three hundred pairs breed in Sicily, Italy, and farther eastward, but it is more common in the Middle East and in Africa. Falcons are predatory birds known for fast aerial pursuit of avian prey, and the amazingly quick Lanner Falcon captures small and midsized birds, especially doves, pigeons, and quail. It also hunts from perches, and consumes rodents, bats, lizards, and insects in addition to birds. Lanner Falcon pairs sometimes stake out a water hole or another wildlife gathering spot and then cooperate to drive, chase, and catch their prey. These falcons inhabit a great variety of habitats, from lowland deserts to forested mountainsides, wherever there are open or lightly wooded hunting sites nearby.

Lanner Falcons vocalize primarily during breeding seasons, and at other times they often appear mostly silent. Their most frequent call is a shrill, piercing *kirrr-kirrr*, *kirrr-rrreee*, or *schreeeee*. Other calls consist of hoarse or rasping cackling sounds. When alarmed near their nests, these falcons utter a long, continuous chatter: *hek-hek-hek-hek-hek*.

GREAT SPOTTED CUCKOO

— Clamator glandarius —

((🐦))
127

Typical harsh vocalizations given by a male Great Spotted Cuckoo.

Cuckoos are known in many parts of the world for their breeding habits. Many cuckoo species, including the Great Spotted Cuckoo, lay their eggs in the nests of other bird species, forcing the involuntary foster parents to raise their young. The Great Spotted Cuckoo, a handsome, generally uncommon species found in Spain, southern France, western Italy, Turkey, Cyprus, and broadly in Africa, seeks out crow and magpie nests to host its eggs. It prefers savanna-like habitats with scattered pine and oak trees, and olive groves. These birds eat insects, such as grasshoppers, termites, moths, and especially large, hairy caterpillars, as well as lizards. Cuckoos often forage for their food on the ground, hopping about in search of prey.

Many cuckoos are noisy birds with loud, sometimes irritating vocalizations, and the *CUCK-ooo* sound of a "cuckoo clock" imitates the call of a European species, the Common Cuckoo. Great Spotted Cuckoos have harsh, cackling calls that often fall in pitch and increase in tempo as they are uttered: *gah-gah-gah . . . gak-gak-gak . . . ko-ko-ko* or *cherr-cherr-che-che-che-che*. A brief call they give when agitated sounds like a nasal *cheh*.

EURASIAN HOOPOE

— Upupa epops —

((🐦))
128

The familiar song of the Eurasian Hoopoe sounds like *poo-poo-poo*.

The Eurasian Hoopoe, a medium-sized, open-country bird, is one of Europe's most distinctive birds. Its magnificent crest, which it usually spreads briefly upon alighting, makes the Eurasian Hoopoe stand out, as do its long, sharp bill and bold coloring. Hoopoes inhabit grasslands, parklands, pastures, vineyards, olive groves, and orchards, either alone or in pairs. They typically forage on the ground for larger insects, spiders, and centipedes, as well as small frogs, lizards, and snakes. Other hoopoes, very similar in appearance to the Eurasian Hoopoe, are found in Africa and Asia.

Eurasian Hoopoe songs, low-pitched and hollow, sound like air being blown into a bottle: *poo-poo-poo* or *oop-oop-oop*. They utter a noisy call when agitated, which sounds like *schaahr* or *scheer*.

LESSER SPOTTED WOODPECKER

— *Dendrocopos minor* —

((129))

The repeated calls, *pee-pee-pee*, of a Lesser Spotted Woodpecker.

Only about six inches long from bill tip to tail tip, the Lesser Spotted Woodpecker is Europe's smallest woodpecker. It is uncommon in many areas but ranges over much of the continent, also occurring eastward through a broad swath of Asia. This shy bird inhabits forests, woodlands, orchards, parks, and tree-filled gardens. It usually searches for insects on tree trunks, smaller branches, and even twigs, where it frequently hangs upside down to better reach hiding prey. Caterpillars are these woodpeckers' favorite summer foods, and they occasionally consume fruits as well.

The Lesser Spotted Woodpecker's territorial call is a shrill series of *kee, pee,* or *piit* notes that slows in tempo near the end: *pee-pee-pee-pee-pee-pee-peee-peee*. A brief call sounds like *pik* or *chik*.

EUROPEAN ROLLER

— Coracias garrulus —

((🐦))
130

A European Roller calls during a territorial display flight.

Rollers are vividly colored birds of Eurasia, Africa, and Australia named for their spectacular, acrobatic aerial displays. In these performances, which are often directed aggressively at territorial intruders, the rollers fly straight up into the air, then dive toward the ground while twisting around, beating their wings, and giving loud calls; near the ground they level off and fly up again to repeat the process. The European Roller, unmistakable with its turquoise head and wing patches, is the continent's only roller species. It lives in the Mediterranean region from Portugal and Spain to Turkey, inhabiting mostly dry, flat or rolling wooded landscapes, including woodland edges, orchards, and agricultural areas with scattered trees. Rollers feed alone or in pairs by perching on high vantage points such as dead tree branches or utility wires and scanning for prey. They take both flying insects and prey from the ground, such as small frogs, lizards, snakes, and mice.

Rollers make harsh, strident, sometimes cawing sounds similar to those of crows. Typical rattle-like calls sound like *rak-rak-rak* or *k-k-k-k-k-k-k-krak-ra*. During their diving, rolling displays, they stretch these calls into a long *rak-rak-rak-rak-rarrarrarrarrarrarr*.

CALANDRA LARK

— Melanocorypha calandra —

Used to attract a mate, the display song flight of a male Calandra Lark.

The Calandra Lark, typical of the lark family, is a superbly camouflaged ground bird that enjoys open-country habitats. It lives in southern Europe as well as the Middle East and northern Africa, frequenting grassy plains, plateaus, and open agricultural areas. In other ways similar to several European lark species, including the famed Common Skylark, the Calandra Lark is distinguished by the black patch on the side of its chest. It forages singly or in small flocks, walking or running along the ground in search of food: insects during spring and summer, and seeds and other plant material in winter.

Like other lark species, male Calandra Larks engage in song flights, during which they circle and hang high in the sky while singing, sometimes for extended periods, before flying away or spiraling back to the ground. These flight displays are probably instrumental in attracting mates or maintaining territories. The song of the male Calandra Lark, given in the air but also sometimes from the ground, is a long medley of rolling trills interspersed with fast, chirpy sounds, like *schreee*, *trip-trip*, or *khitra*.

RUFOUS BUSH ROBIN
— Cercotrichas galactotes —

((🐦))
132

The rich and melodic song of a male Rufous Bush Robin.

The Rufous Bush Robin, also called the Rufous Scrub Robin or Rufous-tailed Scrub Robin, is a pretty little thrush that lives in parts of southern Europe, including Spain, Portugal, and Greece. It breeds in dry, open habitats with dense shrub cover and, when living near people, favors such locales as fruit orchards and hedges. After breeding, this small bird moves to sub-Saharan Africa for the winter. Rufous Bush Robins feed by quickly hopping about on the ground, in search of insects, spiders, worms, and similar prey; they occasionally fly up to pick bugs off short vegetation.

The rich, trilling, twittering, melodic song of the Rufous Bush Robin is sometimes given in flight during a slow, descending aerial display. Calls include a harsh *teck-teck* and a whistling *piu* or *uuh*.

- 245 -

MOUSTACHED WARBLER

— Acrocephalus melanopogon —

((🐦))
133

An example of the advertising song of the male Moustached Warbler.

The Moustached Warbler is a small, highly camouflaged brown bird that lives in waterside environments, instead of among trees like most warblers. It frequents marshes with tall aquatic vegetation, and also borders of lakes, rivers, and streams in southern and central Europe, in particular along the Mediterranean coast. It forages in reedbeds and on muddy banks and floating rafts of vegetation for insects and other small invertebrates. This warbler typically cocks its tail upward or flicks it up and down when agitated.

Observers most frequently hear the Moustached Warbler's brief, throaty call, sounding like *trek* or *trrrt*, as well as an elongated, clicking *trek-tk-tk-tk* sound. Their songs consist of a string of varied notes that usually include *lu-lu-lu-lu* or *vu-vu-vu-vu*.

RED-FLANKED BLUETAIL

— *Tarsiger cyanurus* —

((🐦))
134

The territorial song of the male, sung at dawn.

Quite rare in Europe, where it breeds only in the cool, dense forests of the continent's extreme northeast, the Red-flanked Bluetail is more common in parts of Asia. Also known as Blue-tailed Robin, Orange-flanked Bush Robin, and Siberian Bluestart, this species mostly eats insects that it catches in trees. It also flies down to hunt in low shrubs and hop about in search of prey. In addition to their regular diet, during nonbreeding periods they eat seeds and fruit. After breeding in the far north of Europe, these small, shy birds make an astounding long-distance migration to the south and east, skirting the Himalayas, to winter in southeastern Asia. During this trip, Red-flanked Bluetails inhabit open woodlands, orchards, and even gardens.

At their breeding grounds, male Red-flanked Bluetails often sing at dawn or just before, from the top of a tall tree. Their melancholy songs are a series of fast, thin notes, like *tetee-teeleee-tititi* and *itru-churr-tre-tre-tru-trurr*. Various brief calls of the bluetail include an abrupt, loud *tac* or *tic-tic* and a quiet *huit*.

ORPHEAN WARBLER

— Sylvia hortensis —

(())
135

The male Orphean Warbler uses its song in territorial defense and mate attraction.

This small, plain, secretive bird breeds across a wide stretch of southern Europe, particularly in the Mediterranean region. It prefers warm, dry, open woodlands with brushy undergrowth, but also inhabits shrubby hillsides, hedgerows, olive groves, parkland, gardens, and scrub areas along the coast. These warblers mostly dwell in trees, but they forage from low bushes to high treetops, moving constantly to search for insects on branches and leaves. Orphean Warblers migrate to spend winters in sub-Saharan Africa.

The slow, warbling songs of the Orphean Warbler vary quite a bit in length and kinds of notes used from region to region; some sound like *teero-teero-teero* or *turu turu turu turu . . . liru liru liru tru* or *wee-oo wee-oo wee-oo*. Their short calls include a hard *teck* or *tak* and a rattling *trrrrr* or *churrrr*.

ROCK SPARROW

— Petronia petronia —

((136))

The Rock Sparrow's common call, a trilling *tii-tur'r'r'r*.

The Rock Sparrow, also known as the Rock Petronia, is a small, inconspicuous bird of barren hills and mountains in southern Europe, northern Africa, and parts of central Asia. Mostly a patchy and streaky pale brown, black, and white, they inhabit rocky outcrops, cliffs, ravines, stony desert areas, and archaeological ruin sites. The Rock Sparrow runs and hops along grass and rocks, searching for foods such as seeds, grain, fruit, berries, and insects. Rock Sparrows breed in colonies of up to a hundred pairs, and are also quite gregarious outside the breeding season, when they remain in their flocks.

These vocal birds utter a number of brief, often nasal calls—such as their typical loud, drawn-out *sle-veeit* or *tee-vit*—that may function as a song when repeated several times. Their other calls are a trill-like *tii-tur'r'r'r* and a metallic *pee uoo-ee*.

WESTERN ROCK NUTHATCH

— Sitta neumayer —

((🐦))
137

The song of this species, a series of clear whistles, given by both sexes.

Nuthatches are small, highly agile birds celebrated for their unusual ability to walk both upward and downward—head-first—on tree trunks in search of insects. The Western Rock Nuthatch, a resident of rocky terrain often with cliffs and boulders, uses this skill in its own surroundings to move up and down large rocks and cliff faces. This white and blue-grey bird with a bold eye-stripe is sometimes spotted alone or in small family parties, hopping energetically among rocks on stony hillsides or in ravines or gorges. Western Rock Nuthatches occur in southeastern Europe, from Albania and Greece through Turkey, where visitors can spot them at many ancient, rocky archaeological ruins.

Observers often describe the Western Rock Nuthatch's vocalizations as loud and strident. Their calls include a sharp *chik* and a throaty *schrah*. Both males and females give the species' song, a series of clear whistles and trills that sometimes speeds up and descends in pitch: *itititit . . . toowee toowee toowee* or *vi-YU vi-YU vi-YU . . . tui-tui-tui-tui . . . vivivivivi.*

ALPINE CHOUGH
— *Pyrrhocorax graculus* —

138

A typical call given by an Alpine Chough in flight.

Alpine Choughs are large black birds that swoop and glide along the cliff faces and ridgelines of the high mountains in central and southern Europe, including the Alps and Pyrenees. They are part of the jay and crow family, though differing from crows in their brightly colored bills and legs, among other features. Alpine Choughs are very social, often associating in flocks of a hundred or more that fly together daily to feeding and roosting sites. When foraging, the birds tend to break up into smaller groups or pairs. Their favorite foods are insects and other small invertebrates such as beetles and snails, which they pick up or dig from the ground in grassy or rocky areas. They also eat berries, seeds, and some carrion. These cheeky birds frequently visit alpine ski resorts, where they eat garbage and beg for handouts; ever curious, choughs also follow hikers and accept food from them.

Alpine Choughs produce a number of different calls, many of which are squeaky, chittering, or churring. When in a flock, their frequent calls include a high-pitched *zirrrr*, a piercing *ziieh* or *zeee-up*, and a hissing *chir-rish*. Choughs' other common calls are a sweet-sounding *preeep* and a whistled *sweeeoo*.

TWITE

— Carduelis flavirostris —

((139   ))

Two phrases in the territorial song of a male Twite.

The Twite is a small, streaky, dark finch that lives in open habitats in the United Kingdom, France, Germany, Poland, and Scandinavia, as well as the Middle East and central Asia. During breeding season, they favor open hillsides, moorlands, alpine meadows, and high-elevation plateaus; observers have spotted them on mountains as high as sixteen thousand feet. In autumn, following breeding, Twites descend to lower elevations and spend the winter in river valleys, pasture areas, marshes, lower hillsides, and along the seacoast. Twites forage either on the ground or in low vegetation, hopping along and searching for insects and seeds among weeds or in cultivated fields; they also scavenge at garbage dumps. They are social birds, and typically breed in small colonies and flock in fairly large groups in the autumn and winter.

The Twite is named for its distinctive, nasal, drawn-out *twa-eeet*, *tveeiht*, *tweee* or *chweee*, often given during flight. Its other calls are mixes of twittering notes. The Twite's song, a quick series of buzzes, trills, and twitters, may include some of its "twite" calls.

BLACK-HEADED BUNTING

— Emberiza melanocephala —

140

The song of a male bunting, proceeded by several *zrt* notes.

The Black-headed Bunting, a yellow-and-brown bird with a striking black head, breeds in southeastern Europe, from Italy eastward to Turkey, and in parts of the Middle East. They live in dry, open country, often with scattered bushes or trees, and in thickets and agricultural lands. In late summer and early autumn, these buntings migrate in small flocks to winter in India, and frequently forage in cultivated fields and scrubby areas. Black-headed Buntings mostly eat grass seeds and cereal grains, as well as insects during the breeding season.

The Black-headed Bunting emits a variety of brief, ticking, and occasionally metallic calls, usually sounding like *chlip*, *chleep*, *dzuu*, and *prriu*. It tends to give some calls only in flight, including an abrupt *chup* or *plutt* and a metallic *tzik*. Its melodious yet harsh song, usually given from a high perch such as a tree or utility wire, starts out with *zrt* notes and accelerates with a variety of other notes: *zrt zrt preepree chu-chiwu-chiwu ze-treeeurr.*

AFRICA

Nature enthusiasts who visit Africa thrill to see the continent's large mammals—the zebras, giraffes, elephants, rhinoceroses, and many others. But increasingly, Africa's magnificent birdlife is also a target of international tourism and appreciation. Birdwatchers on wildlife safaris now frequently ask their guides and drivers to stop for viewing not just wildebeest, hippopotamuses, and crocodiles, but wonderful birds such as ibises, storks, and cranes. The storied landscapes of Africa—the deserts, scrubs, grasslands, wooded savannas, and rainforests—support an amazing array of birds, a total of about nineteen hundred species. Four countries each have more than one thousand species within their borders: Tanzania, Kenya, Cameroon, and the Democratic Republic of Congo.

A small number of bird groups that occur only in Africa are especially intriguing. One of these, the turacos, are large, tree-dwelling birds that often have brilliant plumage of blue, green, or purple. Some have interesting names, such as "go-away-bird" and "plantain-eater." The mousebirds and sugarbirds are also restricted to Africa. Mousebirds remind people of mice because they are drably colored and scuttle energetically through their habitats like small rodents as they search for food; sugarbirds are nectar-eating birds of southern Africa that have very long bills and tails. Finally, the Hamerkop, an odd, storklike bird with an anvil-shaped head, is one of the avian world's mysteries—it has no existing close relatives and consequently is usually placed alone in its own bird family.

Africa also has an abundance of birds of prey, as well as many coursers—ground birds that favor running over flying, and honeyguides, one species of which leads people to beehives. Hornbills, with their massive bills and fascinating nesting behavior, are common in Africa, as are kingfishers, barbets, shrikes, starlings, and weavers.

MARABOU STORK

— Leptoptilos crumeniferus —

((🐦))
141

A Marabou Stork's bill-clattering, which it often gives when threatening.

Considered by some to be one of the world's ugliest birds, the Marabou Stork stands about four feet tall and has a very impressive wingspan of up to nine feet. Observers often describe this stork as gaunt-looking because of its nearly featherless red or pink head with dark spots and similarly colored large hanging throat sac. Marabous inhabit much of tropical Africa, where they flourish both in open, dry savanna and grassland and in wetlands such as swamps, riversides, and lake shores. They often forage in groups, both on land and in shallow water. They frequently scavenge at animal carcasses, and they also eat a wide array of live animals, such as fish, frogs, lizards, snakes, mice, rats, and birds as large as flamingos. Marabous also follow herds of the large mammals to catch the insects they scare up.

Marabou Storks are fairly quiet except when breeding and on or near their nests, when they emit a number of different whistling, whining, and grunting calls. They threaten intruders near their nests with *mwaaa* calls. These storks also make clattering sounds with their bills.

AFRICAN WATTLED LAPWING
— *Vanellus senegallus* —

((🐦 142))

A repeated *kip-kip-kip*, the repeated alarm calls of an African Wattled Lapwing.

Ranging over many regions south of the Sahara Desert, the African Wattled Lapwing is a member of the plover shore-bird family. It favors marsh edges and damp grasslands near lakes, ponds, and wet cultivated areas such as flooded rice fields. In pairs or small groups, these long-legged birds slowly walk along, pausing when they spot prey, usually insects or worms. They then step or jump toward the prey and catch it. Grass seeds round out their diet.

These birds emit their alarm call frequently: a repeated *kip-kip-kip* or *ke-WEEP, ke-WEEP, ke-WEEP*. During fights, or when otherwise excited, they give rapid, high-pitched *peep-peep* calls. When the lapwings land on their territories, they often utter a single, loud *peep*.

COQUEREL'S COUA

— Coua coquereli —

(())
143

The loud song of the elusive Coquerel's Coua, a bird more often heard than seen.

A large, slender ground bird found in forests on the western side of Madagascar, the Coquerel's Coua sports a patch of bare blue skin marked with a reddish spot, around each eye. Alone or in pairs, this secretive member of the cuckoo family typically walks about on the forest floor looking for food, and people sometimes see it as it crosses trails. These birds also forage in bushes and small trees, looking for insects, spiders, berries, and fruit. When alarmed, Coquerel's Couas are more likely to run away than to fly.

This coua's most common vocalization is a loud, clear *kewkiw-kewkewkew* or *kewkew-kewkew*. It gives its other frequent call—*ayoo-ew*—from both the ground and elevated perches. It also emits brief, soft grunts.

GREAT BLUE TURACO

— Corythaeola cristata —

((🐦))
144

A series of rattling *kok-kok-kok* notes typical of this species' song.

The twenty-plus turaco species are all confined to the African continent, where they prefer forests, woodlands, and savannas. These large, tree-dwelling birds have long been hunted for their brilliantly colored feathers. The Great Blue Turaco, the largest of the family, has exquisite coloring; it is one of Africa's loveliest birds. A resident of the rain forests of Central and West Africa, Great Blues usually congregate in small groups of three to seven. They feed all day, especially during the early evening, eating various fruits, leaves, flowers, and tree buds. When they finish foraging in one tree, they fly to the next in single file, one bird after another gliding from tree to tree.

The raucous, often repetitive calls of turacos are some of the most characteristic sounds of the areas in which they live. The common long call of the Great Blue Turaco starts with trilling *prru . . . prru . . .* or *roh-ou* notes that change to a long series of rattling *kok-kok-kok-kok* sounds, and sometimes end with several *ta-tek* notes.

SPECKLED MOUSEBIRD

— *Colius striatus* —

((🐦))
145

Several common calls given by a foraging Speckled Mousebird.

The Speckled Mousebird is one of six mousebird species, all of which are restricted to Africa. They are known as mousebirds not because they feed on rodents, but because of their drab, long-tailed appearance and their habits of scuttling through vegetation and huddling together in a tight group of four to eight when resting or sleeping. Larger groups may gather together at good food sources. Found in many regions south of the Sahara, Speckled Mousebirds mostly consume fruit, but also buds, flowers, and nectar. They live in a variety of habitats, from thickets to open woodlands to forest edges. These mousebirds also live in parks and gardens and eat cultivated fruits, vegetables, and flowers, giving them a bad reputation among farmers and gardeners.

Mousebirds are very vocal, but many people consider their raspy calls to be scratchy and unpleasant. One of the Speckled Mousebird's common calls, perhaps given to stay in contact with members of their flock, sounds like *chew-chew* or *siu-siu*. Their other calls include a sharp *tsi-ui* given just before flying and a *tru . . . tru . . .* call emitted in flight. They utter a strident *schiech* and an explosive *pit* as alarm calls.

WHITE-FRONTED BEE-EATER
— *Merops bullockoides* —

((146))

The calls of a pair of White-fronted Bee-eaters, given from a nest hole.

Bee-eaters live in the warm climates of southern Europe, southern Asia, Africa, and Australia. However, most of the species inhabit Africa, including the very attractive White-fronted Bee-eater. These elegant, brilliantly colored birds feed by catching and eating bees with their long, thin bills. In fact, bees, wasps, and hornets—which they can handle relatively safely with their bills—make up about eighty percent of their diet, with other insects such as beetles, flies, butterflies, and grasshoppers making up the remainder. White-fronted Bee-eaters associate in small groups but often separate during the day to hunt alone. The birds perch on tree branches or bushes and upon spotting an appropriate insect, fly out to catch it, then return to a resting spot to eat it. White-fronted Bee-eaters often live in woodlands along rivers or lakes, but also in other habitats with trees or bushes. They inhabit eastern and central Africa south to parts of southern Africa.

The White-fronted Bee-eater is quite a vocal bird, with a variety of brief calls. It most frequently gives a deep, muffled *gaaar* or *gaauu*. Other calls, which may rise or fall in pitch, sound like *kwannk*, *krrrt*, *kakaka*, and *waaru*.

LILAC-BREASTED ROLLER
— *Coracias caudatus* —

147

The repeated *rak-rak-rak* calls of a brilliant Lilac-breasted Roller, given during a display flight.

Rollers are striking, colorful birds with relatively large heads and short necks. In most regions of Africa outside the Sahara Desert, they are often seen perching conspicuously in trees. One of the most beautiful is the Lilac-breasted Roller, which hails from the eastern and southern portions of the continent. The species has a reputation as an aggressive defender of its breeding territories, diving at intruders—including people—that dare to enter. Like other rollers, they give amazing flight displays in which males plunge toward the ground, then level off quickly and roll left and right, all the while shrieking loudly. Usually spotted alone or in pairs, Lilac-breasted Rollers mainly live in dry, open woodlands and grassy savannas with scattered trees. They feed by swooping down from an elevated perch on a wide variety of animal prey, including insects, spiders, scorpions, snails, frogs, lizards, and small birds. They swallow small creatures whole while on the ground, and beat and dismember larger animals before consuming them at their perch.

During their display flights, Lilac-breasted Rollers first give a loud, rasping *rak* that is repeated many times—*rak-rak-rak-rak* . . . —leading into a series of rattles, like *kaaa, kaarsh, kaaaaarrsh*.

GREEN WOOD HOOPOE

— Phoeniculus purpureus —

((🐦))
148

The raucous cackling of a group of Green Wood Hoopoes is a common sound on African savannas.

The Green Wood Hoopoe is a striking tree dweller, with highly iridescent coloring and a long, bright, down-curved bill. It usually moves about in families of four to eight. It lives in a variety of wooded and forested lands, especially savannas and open woodlands, in central and southern Africa. This species requires large trees to thrive because it feeds in trees, and sleeps and nests in tree cavities. Green Wood Hoopoes forage acrobatically on tree trunks and branches, frequently hanging upside-down or at odd angles to probe bark and crevices for prey. Their sharp bills hammer at the bark to pry it away in search of hiding insects, spiders, centipedes, and millipedes. The birds also eat small lizards and some fruits.

Green Wood Hoopoes often engage in cackling group displays. During these displays, known as "rallies," the wood hoopoe group gathers at one of its territorial boundaries. All the birds perch close together, rock back and forth, and give prolonged chuckling or bubbling vocalizations that sound like *kak-kak-kkkkk*. All Green Wood Hoopoe vocalizations differ slightly between the sexes; for example, males emit *kuk* as their alarm call, whereas females produce *ke-ek*.

TRUMPETER HORNBILL

— Bycanistes bucinator —

((149))

The common wailing call of a group of Trumpeter Hornbills, given from the canopy of an African forest.

Hornbills are some of the world's most extraordinary birds, notable for their immense bills and for their unique breeding practices—the female secludes herself in a tree cavity to incubate eggs and feed her young, and her mate feeds her through a small hole. The Trumpeter Hornbill is a denizen of forests and woodlands, especially near water. Groups of thirty to forty birds often spend nights together; at sunrise they head off in smaller groups to forage in trees for the day. They eat mainly fruit, particularly figs, but they also consume insects, crabs, and small birds and nestlings. Despite their large size, these uncommon hornbills are excellent flyers, their flight paths twisting and turning through tree canopies. Trumpeter Hornbills range from Kenya south to Mozambique and parts of South Africa, and westward to Angola.

The characteristic call of the Trumpeter Hornbill is a prolonged, braying vocalization that loses energy and dies away at the end, like a wailing *naaay-naaaaaaay-naaaaaaay-naaaay* or *nhaa nhaahahahaha*. During feeding, the hornbills usually utter low, guttural clucking, grunting, or croaking sounds.

RED-AND-YELLOW BARBET

— Trachyphonus erythrocephalus —

((🐦))
150

A pair of Red-and-Yellow Barbets duet a repeated *teedle-kwau*.

The Red-and-yellow Barbet is easily one of the most stunning smaller birds of East Africa. With its colorful head and chest and black-and-white patterning, this species stands out in the open woodlands and wooded grasslands it favors. Red-and-yellow Barbets associate in pairs or small family groups of three to ten. They often forage along the ground, looking for fruits—especially figs—seeds, insects, spiders, and small birds and their eggs. They also sometimes feed on trash and pick dead insects from automobile radiator grills. Red-and-yellow Barbets often burrow into termite mounds to nest.

Birdwatchers love barbets not only for their good looks but for their melodic singing. Red-and-yellow Barbets are known for their spectacular loud duets, during which a paired male and female erupt into waves of precisely coordinated, repeated vocalizations. The male utters three whistled notes and the female joins in with three to five higher-pitched short notes that fit in with the male's notes. The result sounds like a minute or two of a repeated *teedle-kwau, teedle-kwau, teedle-kwau*; or, as some describe it, *red'n yell-ow, red'n yell-ow, red'n yell-ow*.

GREATER HONEYGUIDE
— Indicator indicator —

151

The Greater Honeyguide's song, a repeated *wi-chew*, often given for hours.

The Greater Honeyguide is a rather drab-looking brown bird that eats bees, termites, ants, and flies—and loves beeswax, the yellow substance secreted by bees for building honeycombs. It prefers the open woodlands and woodland edges of sub-Saharan Africa, but is also found in streamside woods and farmlands with scattered trees. The Greater Honeyguide is famous for leading people to honeybee hives. The guiding is mutually advantageous: people procure honey, and the guides, by tradition, are left some of the beeswax after the humans break into the hive. A bird catches the attention of a honey hunter by giving a distinctive "guiding call" from a tree. As the person approaches the bird, it flies to the next tree closer to the beehive, and continues calling there, and so on until they reach the hive.

The Greater Honeyguide's guiding call is a noisy, nasal chattering sound, sometimes combined with various peeping or piping notes. Males usually give the species' song: soft *peew* notes followed by a series of notes like *wi-chew* or *tor-vik*. Males also emit an aggressive *freeeeer*.

EASTERN NICATOR

— Nicator gularis —

((🐦))
152

The Eastern Nicator's conspicuous song is often the only clue to its presence.

The three species of nicators, which look quite similar, are mysterious both because ornithologists have trouble classifying them and because they are secretive, usually staying concealed in dense vegetation. They are heard often but are spotted only infrequently. The Eastern Nicator is patchily distributed in several regions of forests, woodlands, and thickets in eastern and southern Africa. They search for their prey, insects such as beetles and caterpillars, by hopping leisurely about branches within tree canopies, sometimes descending to the ground.

The Eastern Nicator is very vocal, typically singing its loud songs from hidden perches. Its songs start with a low *yik-chop weeoo-tok trrr* or *yu-ik-wit-wer-trr* and then proceed into a jumbled whistling, like *cho-chou-choou-chueeee* or *hip-to-wee-to-chip to-weet*. Its common call is a sharp *tuk*, and its alarm call sounds like *tsuck* or *zokk*.

WHITE-BROWED ROBIN-CHAT

— *Cossypha heuglini* —

((🐦))
153

The beautiful song of a male White-browed Robin-Chat.

The White-browed Robin-Chat, a robinlike bird with a bold white eye-stripe, is found in many habitats in eastern and southern Africa, although it avoids dense forests. It seems to prefer areas near water and even moves into parks and gardens. Usually spotted alone or in pairs, White-browed Robin-Chats often emerge from dense vegetation around dusk to forage on open ground. They move around with quick, bounding hops, catching insects such as ants, termites, and beetles, and sometimes flipping over leaves with their bills to look for hiding prey.

Bird lovers consider robin-chats fine singers. Males give the species' distinctive song, a repeated refrain of a few high notes followed by a few low notes, which increases in volume and tempo with each repetition. One such song sounds like *trickle-chok-twee* or *wuut wuut chero-chiii*.

BLACK-THROATED APALIS

— Apalis jacksoni —

((🐦))
154

The repeated *t'link-t'link-t'link* is a typical male Black-throated Apalis song.

The tiny, attractive Black-throated Apalis is a member of a large family of warblerlike birds that also includes prinias and cisticolas, and that is distributed throughout Africa, Eurasia, and Australia. This crisp-looking apalis inhabits only higher-elevation forests in scattered parts of central and eastern Africa. It typically associates in pairs or small family groups of three to four. These active birds hop along the branches of trees, rooting about twigs and leaves for insects and spiders and swooping after flying insects. They stay mainly within the tree canopy, often at middle levels.

The Black-throated Apalis produces a musical, metallic-sounding song of simple pure notes—*t'link-t'link-t'link*—which they sometimes continue for a long period. Their other vocalizations include a soft, plaintive *piu* or *pu* sound.

BLACK-THROATED WATTLE-EYE

— Platysteira peltata —

((🐦))
155

The song, *djip-djip-zipweet, zipweet, zipweet,* of a male Black-throated Wattle-eye.

Wattle-eyes, known for the rings of brightly colored bare skin around their eyes, are small flycatcher-like birds that live only in Africa. The rare Black-throated Wattle-eye, with its broad bill and conspicuous red eye wattle, resides in forests and woodlands, mainly in the southern and eastern regions of the continent. These generally quiet birds are found flitting about tree foliage, foraging for insects. They often rapidly open and close their wings, which may help them flush bugs from hiding spots. Black-throated Wattle-eyes usually associate in pairs or small family parties.

Black-throated Wattle-eye mated pairs often duet. The songs, which vary a bit regionally, sound raspy or scratchy and unmusical, like *djip-djip-djip-djip-zipweet, zipweet, zipweet, zipweet* or *ch ch ch ch . . . in-cherin-cherin-cherin-cherinch.* The species' alarm call is *tsit-tsit.*

VARIABLE SUNBIRD

— Cinnyris venustus —

((156))

A typical song given by a male Variable Sunbird.

Sunbirds, which remind many birdwatchers of hummingbirds, are small birds with long, down-curved bills that help them draw nectar from flowers; the Variable Sunbird is an exquisite, iridescent example. It ranges through many regions of western, eastern, and southern Africa and inhabits a variety of environments, including forests, woodlands, savannas, mangroves, and gardens. The species was probably named the Variable Sunbird because males during their breeding season vary in appearance, depending on the region: birds in parts of Ethiopia have a white belly, in Mozambique a yellow belly, and in Uganda an orange-and-yellow belly. This sunbird is very active as it searches leaves and flowers for insects and spiders and takes nectar from flowers, sometimes hovering to do so. It also catches flying insects in the air.

Male Variable Sunbirds sit on exposed perches, spread their tails, and sing. Like their belly colors, the songs of this species vary regionally, but usually consist of two to seven introductory notes followed by a rattling chatter, like *tsweuip-tsweuip-tsweuip-tsweuip-chatatatatatatatata* or *te-tch-weee te-tch-weee te-tch-weee cha-cha-cha-cha-cha-cha-cha*. The species' common brief calls are *chip* and *chop*, and mates frequently twitter at each other with a repeated *zi-zi-zi-zi*.

CAPE SUGARBIRD

— Promerops cafer —

((🐦))
157

A typical call, a repeated *chit* note.

The two species of sugarbirds, which are long-tailed songbirds, are found only in southern Africa, and are sometimes used as symbols of the wildlife of this beautiful region. The Cape Sugarbird, the male of which has an extremely long, wispy tail, lives only in South Africa, in the southern portion of the country. This bird's life is intimately tied to a single type of plant: a group of shrubs known as proteas. From these plants the birds obtain food, shelter, nest sites, and nest materials. Cape Sugarbirds, which generally associate in pairs or small family groups, perch on protea flowers and use their long, thin bills and sucking tongues to draw nectar from the flowers. They also eat spiders and small insects such as beetles and flies that they find on the flowers.

The Cape Sugarbirds' songs are long and complex, composed of scratchy, grating notes, as well as some notes that are more liquid-sounding. These are all usually interspersed with hard *chit* notes, like *tschaak-tschayli-chitchit, tchit-tsch-aluwit-tscheeluwo-cho, tschaak-tscha-witchi-chut*. Its brief calls include a tinny *tcheenk-tcheenk* and a rapid *skwidge-skwidge* or *skeedge-skeedge*; alarm calls sound like *tweet-tweet* or a harsh, wheezing *sssssrrrr*.

SUPERB STARLING

— Lamprotornis superbus —

((🐦))
158

A portion of the rambling song of a male Superb Starling.

Many starling species inhabit Africa, and the glossy Superb Starling, with its deep-blue breast, is one of the prettiest. A very social bird that often associates in small flocks, the Superb Starling is distributed over much of eastern Africa, from Ethiopia south to Tanzania. It lives in open habitats in arid and semi-arid areas, including open woodlands, savannas, and grasslands. During the warmest portion of the day these birds rest in leafy trees, but at other times they forage on the ground. Their diet consists mostly of insects, but they also eat fruit, berries, flowers, and seeds.

The songs of Superb Starlings are long and rambling, consisting of a wide variety of notes. Some parts of these songs usually sound like *weeoo-chu* and a down-slurred *cheeooo*. Excited birds often utter a long call, like *whit-chor-chi-vii*. Their alarm call is *chirrrr*.

RED-BILLED OXPECKER

— *Buphagus erythrorhynchus* —

((🐦))
159

Typical calls, *tsssssaaaa* and *tsik-tsik*, given by a flock of Red-billed Oxpeckers.

Africa's two species of oxpeckers are starling relatives with an interesting but somewhat distasteful lifestyle: They spend almost all day perched on large, grazing mammals, picking and eating the ticks, lice, leeches, and other blood-sucking parasites that infest the mammals. Red-billed Oxpeckers have sharp, curved claws that help them cling to the hairy hides of such favored hunting grounds as giraffes, rhinoceroses, buffalos, and zebras. Although they usually congregate in groups of four to eight, up to twenty of these gregarious birds may gather on a single large mammal. Red-billed Oxpeckers range from Eritrea south to northern South Africa.

Red-billed Oxpeckers utter a number of long, sharp hissing calls: *zzhaaaaa*, *ssshhhhh*, and *tssssaaaa*. They often accompany these calls with clicking sounds, such as *tsik-tsik* or *trik-trik*.

PIN-TAILED WHYDAH

— Vidua macroura —

((🐦))
160

A few notes from the advertising song of a male.

Whydahs, small African finches, are known for their splendid long tails and for their unusual breeding. They are brood parasites, which means they do not nest, but rather lay their eggs in the nests of other species, which then incubate their eggs and raise their young. The elegant Pin-tailed Whydah prefers to place its eggs in the nests of other small finches called waxbills. The Pin-tailed Whydah ranges across most of sub-Saharan Africa, where it prefers grassy and open shrubby habitats, as well as woodlands, agricultural areas, and gardens. Whydahs live mainly on grass seeds, kicking aside topsoil with their feet and then picking up exposed seeds. They also occasionally catch flying termites. Only male Pin-tailed Whydahs have a long tail, during the breeding season; females are brown, plain-looking, and sparrowlike.

Pin-tailed Whydah songs are composed of uneven series of single notes, like *tsip*, *tse-tsuc*, *tyap*, *tsrrr*, *wee*, *tip*, *jaa*. Sometimes they incorporate squeaks and chirps, or whistles such as *tee-yew*. Both males and females produce harsh chattering sounds, and males especially chatter at territorial intruders: *whit-whit-whit* or *chee-chee-chee*. Pin-tailed Whydahs in flight often utter a sharp *chip-chip!*

ASIA

Asia supports an amazing variety of birds—more than two thousand species. Much of this diversity lies in the tropical belt of southern Asia, from Pakistan and India in the west to southern China and Southeast Asia in the east, and the birds detailed here are concentrated in this region. Environments characteristic of this area include deciduous, evergreen, and swamp forests, and also bamboo habitats, grasslands, scrub, and various wetlands.

Leafbirds, fairy-bluebirds, and ioras are the only types of birds found in this region and nowhere else. All three groups are composed of striking tree-dwellers. Leafbirds are a beautiful, bright leaf-green, fairy-bluebirds a shiny, stunning blue and black, and ioras are yellow and green. Several other bird groups, although not restricted to Asia, are nonetheless quite characteristic of the Asian continent, especially in the south. These include the pheasants, which are very diverse and often especially gaudy in Asia. Some of these pheasants, such as the widely recognized Peafowl (known usually as the pea-cock and pea-hen) and the lesser-known Great Argus, have extremely long, decorative tails and can be more than six feet long overall.

Hornbills, also common in Africa, are plentiful in Asia, and their large size and extraordinary bills render them one of the most compelling bird types of the continent. Parrots, although not as common or diverse as on some of the other continents, are present here, as are trogons, handsomely colored, compact arboreal birds with short necks and long tails. Finally, Asia has a large number of babblers, very noisy, usually gregarious birds with names such as laughingthrush, mesia, and leiothrix.

GERMAIN'S PEACOCK-PHEASANT

— *Polyplectron germaini* —

((161))

The rattling call of this species does not reflect its shy nature.

Germain's Peacock-Pheasant is a rare, secretive, medium-sized pheasant that occupies parts of southern Vietnam and eastern Cambodia. A grey-brown color overall, this chickenlike bird has dull red facial skin and plumage decorated with many bluish and green "ocelli," or eye-like markings. It lives in moist bamboo forests at low and middle elevations. A terrestrial forager, the Germain's Peacock-Pheasant looks for food by strolling slowly and quietly across the forest floor, scratching the ground with its feet and turning over pieces of leaf litter. The species consumes a wide range of foods, including fruits, berries, leaves, shoots, and small animals such as insects and snails. It occurs in only a few scattered localities, and its populations are threatened by hunting and by development of its habitat for agriculture.

The vocal behavior of the shy and retiring Germain's Peacock-Pheasant is not well studied. Males give a series of rattling calls that have been described as purring or growling. They repeat these calls many times, and the calls sometimes grow louder and harsher with succeeding repetitions. One observer described these calls as *erraarrrrrakak . . . aarrrr-akh-akh-akh-akh . . . AKH-AKH-AKH-AKH.*

CRESTED SERPENT EAGLE

— *Spilornis cheela* —

((🐦))
162

The contact call of a Crested Serpent Eagle responding to its mate.

The Crested Serpent Eagle frequently soars over the forests and wooded areas of southern Asia, from India east to the Pacific coast. It varies somewhat in size, but its body is always a dark brownish color; its head is topped by a short, bushy crest that it erects when alarmed. A resident of forests, woodlands, savannas, mangroves, and tree plantations, the Crested Serpent Eagle is usually solitary or part of a pair. As its name implies, this bird often eats snakes, which can be up to three feet long. It sits on exposed perches near forest edges and clearings or along waterways, keenly eying the surrounding trees and ground for prey. When it spots a snake or any of its other prey such as lizards, frogs, crabs, and small birds and mammals, the eagle quickly flies down to snatch its food.

Crested Serpent Eagles are very vocal raptors, producing a variety of loud, clear, ringing calls, including whistles and screams. When pairs soar high above wooded areas, they usually call back and forth to each other. One common call is a duet—one bird begins with a repeated *hurLEEoo*, and the other responds with a lower-pitched *hurLOO-LOO-LOO*.

ALEXANDRINE PARAKEET
— Psittacula eupatria —

((🐦))
163

A foraging parakeet gives two calls, *kee-ah* and *kee-aar*.

The Alexandrine Parakeet, distinguished by its bright red bill and pink-red neck band, is a medium-sized parrot with a long tail that ranges from Pakistan and eastern Afghanistan to portions of Southeast Asia. It makes its home in lowland forests and most other wooded areas, including mangroves, tree plantations, and parks. These birds usually mingle in small groups during the day, but at night they gather in the hundreds, and sometimes in the thousands, to roost communally in large, leafy trees. At dawn they depart the roost with incredible screeching sounds to begin the day's activities. The Alexandrine Parakeet eats fruits such as guavas, seeds, flowers, flower nectar, and some new leaves. It also raids orchards and crop fields for food, sometimes causing considerable damage. Unfortunately, populations of these beautiful birds are declining rapidly in some areas, particularly in Southeast Asia, where people capture an increasing number for the pet trade.

The Alexandrine Parakeet is known for the loud, harsh, screaming sounds it often produces while flying, which typically sound like *kee-ah*, *kee-ak*, or *kee-aar*. Other commonly voiced calls are a loud, raucous *trrr-ieuw* and a cracking *gr-raak . . . gr-raak*.

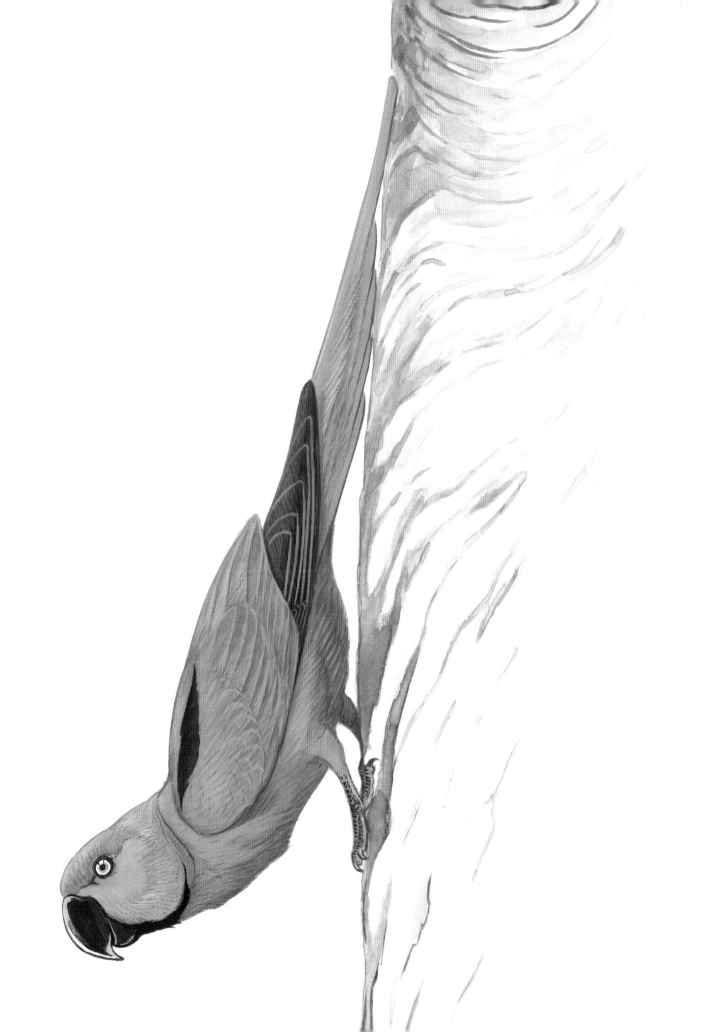

WARD'S TROGON

— Harpactes wardi —

164

The song of a Ward's Trogon consists of rapidly repeated *klu* notes.

The Ward's Trogon is a stunning species whose range is restricted mainly to mountainous regions from Bhutan and northeastern India to Myanmar, southwestern China, and northwestern Vietnam. These fairly rare birds inhabit tall, vine-thick forests and bamboo groves. They eat large insects such as moths, grasshoppers, and stick insects, as well as fruit, berries, and big seeds. Like other trogon species, Ward's Trogons spend most of their time alone or in pairs. They are shy, but they do not always fly away immediately if they see humans. Whereas males are greyish with a maroon tinge and have red patches, females are olive brownish with yellow patches.

When observers are present, Ward's Trogons are usually silent. However, these birds do have several calls, the most frequent being a series of rapid, rich, mellow notes, *klu-klu-klu-klu*, which accelerate and also change slightly in pitch. A harsh call that may serve as an alarm sounds like *whirr-ur*. These trogons also utter a squirrel-like chattering call on occasion.

GREAT BARBET
— Megalaima virens —

((165))

Given by both sexes, the alarm call of this species is a harsh *keeah*.

Barbets occur on several continents and are among the globe's most glamorous birds—they are beautiful, exotic, and often fabulous singers. The Great Barbet, which ranges from northeastern Pakistan and northwestern India to eastern China and parts of Southeast Asia, is the largest species in the barbet family; with its magnificent colors, large, stout bill, and husky silhouette, it is truly a distinctive bird. Great Barbets occupy forests and wooded valleys, often on mountain slopes. They are usually alone or in pairs during breeding seasons, but they congregate in groups of up to thirty or more at food sources during nonbreeding periods. Barbets are fruit-eaters, and the Great Barbet favors such fruits as figs and wild plums. It also eats berries, flower parts, and tree buds, and has a taste for insects as well.

Male and female Great Barbets sing frequently throughout the breeding season, often simultaneously or one after another in duets. Sometimes Great Barbet songs are heard all day, especially near dusk; these are some of the most characteristic sounds of some Himalayan forests. The typical male song consists of series of loud, strident notes, *kee-aar, kay-oh*, and *peeao*; females give rapid *piou-piou-piou* notes. An alarm call is a harsh, grating *keeah*.

RHINOCEROS HORNBILL

— Buceros rhinoceros —

((🐦))
166

A typical honking call from a Rhinoceros Hornbill in the rainforest canopy.

For birders traveling to Southeast Asia, one of the most sought-after sightings is a glimpse of the Rhinoceros Hornbill, found only in peninsular Thailand and Malaysia, Sumatra, Java, and Borneo. Aptly named, this bird is very large, with an amazing, mostly hollow, upturned "casque" atop its huge bill. It usually breeds in pairs and associates in small groups after breeding season ends; however, some observers have spotted flocks as large as twenty or more. Hornbills are primarily fruit-eaters, and the Rhinoceros Hornbill favors the many species of figs native to its rainforest habitat. They also eat insects, tree frogs, lizards, and bird eggs, plucking these foods mainly from trees but also from the ground. Currently, these splendid birds survive only in areas where there are still plenty of large, old trees, in which they roost and nest.

When preparing to fly, Rhinoceros Hornbills utter *ger-honk* or *ger-ronk* calls, which often continue after the birds take off. While they are perched, mated male-female pairs often voice duets that consist of deep, forceful sounds: Males give *hok* notes and the females respond with higher-pitched *hak* notes; in combination, their call sounds like *hok-hak, hok-hak, hok-hak*.

GREATER GOLDENBACK

— Chrysocolaptes lucidus —

167

The Greater Goldenback's most typical call, a metallic rattle.

A handsome woodpecker with a pointed red crest and long bill, the Greater Goldenback is particularly notable for the exquisite black-and-white patterns on its neck and underparts. Also commonly called the Greater Flameback, this species lives in Nepal, India, and eastward into southern China, Southeast Asia, and the Philippines. It prefers forests and their periphery, as well as mangroves, but it also frequents old, decaying tree plantations, such as those that formerly produced teak or rubber. Greater Goldenbacks, generally associating in pairs or family parties, forage almost always in large trees, both living and dead, and only very occasionally come to the ground. They peck and hammer away at wood to excavate holes, in search of caterpillars, ants, the larvae of wood-boring beetles, and various other insects.

Greater Goldenbacks typically utter a brief, single *keek* or *kik* call, but they are better known for producing a rapid, somewhat metallic-sounding rattle, like *tibit-titititit* or *kilkilkitkitkitkit*. Another frequent vocalization, often given in flight, is a series of *kowk-kowk* or *ke-dew-kow* notes; they also emit a staccato *tyu-tyu-tyu* while flying. When two Greater Goldenbacks are near each other, they sometimes produce a series of notes like *t-wuit-wuit*.

BANDED PITTA

— Pitta guajana —

((🐦))
168

The Banded Pitta gives a series of explosive *pouw* notes—a territorial vocalization—from the forest floor.

Although relatively little is known about them, pittas are some of the most gorgeous of the world's birds, and often among the favorites of globe-trotting birdwatchers. Different species are found in Africa, southern Asia, and Australia, but the Banded Pitta, one of the most strikingly marked, occurs only in Thailand, Malaysia, and Indonesia. Banded Pittas inhabit lowland forests, typically with limestone cliffs nearby. Like other pittas, they are shy and elusive. Their wonderful coloring is usually difficult to appreciate because they remain primarily on the dark forest floor. Banded Pittas walk on the ground in search of prey, occasionally scratching the leaf litter with their feet, looking for insects such as ants, termites, caterpillars, and beetles. They also consume earthworms, snails, and some berries. Populations of this beautiful species are, unfortunately, declining rapidly due to habitat destruction and the bird's popularity in the local pet trade.

Banded Pittas are much more often heard than seen. Their vocalizations vary a bit depending on the region, but a typical call is a descending, slightly explosive *pouw*, *poww*, or *hwow*, repeated at brief intervals. These birds also make short whirring sounds, like *kirrr* or *pprrr*, perhaps when they are alarmed; some observers have noted a soft *whup* call as well.

ASIAN FAIRY-BLUEBIRD

— Irena puella —

((169))

The *QUIT-QUIT* call of an alarmed Asian Fairy-bluebird.

The Asian Fairy-bluebird is one of southern Asia's most radiant birds. The males' glossy, deep black-and-blue bodies are brilliant against their usual setting in leafy green tree canopies, so they are easy to spot. Females are a duller blue-green shade overall. A species of tropical and subtropical forests, the sturdy-looking Asian Fairy-bluebird is found from India to Southeast Asia, including many of Indonesia's islands. These comely birds often occur alone or in flocks of up to seven or eight, usually in the middle to upper levels of trees. They are fruit-eaters, grabbing small to medium-sized fruits while they are perched or while flying through foliage; they sometimes consume flower nectar as well. Asian Fairy-bluebirds also pursue and catch flying termites. The species frequently forages in tree canopies in mixed-species flocks.

Vocalizations of Asian Fairy-bluebirds consist mainly of loud, whistling or fluid-like notes. Their songs sound like *do-re-me-hew-hew-hew* and *tu-lip, wae-waet-oo*. These birds have many calls, some of which contain explosive whip-crack sounds, like *QUIT-QUIT!* They utter a number of softer calls while foraging in dense foliage, some of which sound like *weet-weet* and *what's-it*.

SCARLET MINIVET

— *Pericrocotus flammeus* —

((🐦))
170

The song of the Scarlet Minivet.

A dazzling bird, the Scarlet Minivet is a favorite of birdwatchers, not just for the male's bright orange-red and black coloring, but also for its energetic personality. These small birds, which have long tails and rather upright perching postures, range from India, including the Himalayan region, through Southeast Asia to the Philippines. Females are a vibrant yellow and gray. During nonbreeding periods of the year they flit about tree canopies in flocks of up to thirty birds, creating spectacular scenes when they fly and reveal their pretty tail and wing color patterns. In addition to forest areas, Scarlet Minivets inhabit orchards and parks with many tall trees. They primarily eat insects, such as cicadas, grasshoppers, crickets, and caterpillars, which they locate in tree foliage or chase after in the air. These birds also visit trees with ripe fruit, probably to catch insects attracted to the sweetness of the fruit, and hover briefly over flowers to search for hiding bugs.

Scarlet Minivet songs are usually fairly simple, composed of clear, rich, piercing whistles. Various descriptions characterize them as *weep-weep-weep-wit-wip*, or *sweep-sweep-sweep-sweep*, or *swEEET-swEEET-swEEET*. Some of this species' calls are single repetitions of song notes, such as *sweep*.

RED-VENTED BULBUL

— *Pycnonotus cafer* —

((🐦 171))

A male Red-vented Bulbul's typical song.

Mostly tropical songbirds common to many parts of Asia and Africa, bulbuls are highly versatile, as indicated by their successful habitation of regions outside their native ranges, where people have introduced them. The Red-vented Bulbul, which naturally inhabited southern Asia only, now also lives on many Pacific Islands, including Fiji and Hawaii. These birds prefer dry, open habitats, such as scrub and grass areas, orchards, gardens, and roadsides, where they forage in pairs or small groups, often in trees or bushes. They eat primarily fruits, but also some insects and nectar.

Because of their fine vocal abilities, bulbuls are popular cage birds in areas where they live. Red-vented Bulbul songs sound something like *kreink-ker-grr*, *be-quick-quick*, or *be-care-ful*. Calls include a continuous *peep-peep-peep* sound and a harsh *tik-jhurrhh*.

WHITE-THROATED FANTAIL

—Rhipidura albicollis —

((🐦))
172

The typical male song during the breeding season.

Fantails are a group of small, insect-catching birds of Asia and Australasia, named for the way they repeatedly spread their tail feathers into a fan shape as they forage. The purpose of their constant tail movements is probably to scare hiding insects and flush them into the open where the birds can see and catch them. White-throated Fantails, highly active birds of forests, bamboo areas, and wooded gardens, range from Pakistan and India to China and Southeast Asia. They tend to forage in the middle levels of tree canopies, usually near the main tree trunks.

White-throated Fantail songs are typically well-spaced sequences of pretty whistles or tinkling sounds, like *tri riri riri riri riri* or *tsu sit tsu sit sit sit sit-tsu*. Brief calls are squeaky and abrupt—*cheek*, *jick*, *wick*, and *squit*.

GREATER RACKET-TAILED DRONGO

— Dicrurus paradiseus —

((🐦 173))

The Greater Racket-tailed Drongo's typical loud call.

The spectacular Greater Racket-tailed Drongo is truly an unusual sight for bird-watchers in Asia. It has a glossy, black body crowned with a helmetlike crest and amazing, wire-like tail extensions with pendant-shaped endings. The drongos' elaborate tails, in conjunction with their long, pointed wings, may increase their aerial maneuverability, enhancing their ability to catch flying insects. Greater Racket-tailed Drongos range from India and Sri Lanka to China and Southeast Asia. They are forest-dwelling birds, but they also visit tree plantations. They forage for a wide variety of insects, from small flies to large butterflies and beetles, in the middle and lower levels of forests, often joining other birds to form mixed-species feeding flocks. A bold bird, the Greater Racket-tailed Drongo sometimes attacks much larger birds that come too close to it, including huge hornbills.

Songs of Greater Racket-tailed Drongos are loud and varied, sometimes musical and whistling, other times screechy and churring, or metallic and bell-like. In one region the songs consist of a few jerky notes, which sound like *tu-whit*, *clee-uw*, *tu-whit*, *clee-uw*. Some longer calls resemble a whistling *vit-vit-vit* or a bell-like *clink-link-link*.

COMMON IORA

—*Aegithina tiphia* —

((174))

The song of a Common Iora, used to attract a mate.

Ioras are small, greenish-and-yellow birds of southern Asia that flit energetically and acrobatically about tree foliage as they forage. The very pretty Common Iora is native to southern China, Southeast Asia, and India. It prefers to live in open forests, forest edges, tree plantations, wooded roadsides, mangroves, and parks. Usually alone or in pairs, these ioras hop methodically through trees and bushes, searching mainly for fruits. They frequently hang upside down from twigs to reach choice items, including some insects. Females are often a bit more pale-colored than males.

Common Iora pairs typically call back and forth to each other as they forage. Many of the calls are whistles, some sounding like *di-di-dwiu dwi-o dwi-o dwi-o* and *di-du di-du*; another kind of call sounds like *chee-chit-chit-chit*. Simple songs of this species include a long, drawn-out note followed by a much lower-pitched note, *whiiiii-piu* or *wheeee-teoo*.

BLUETHROAT

— Luscinia svecica —

((🐦))
175

The rambling breeding song of a Bluethroat.

The Bluethroat, a small, pretty bird with a bright blue bib, populates parts of four continents, from South and East Asia to northern Africa, and Europe and Alaska. It is often secretive, typically foraging on or near the ground. On long legs, it runs and hops about in paddy fields, scrub areas, tall grass, and shrubbery along watercourses. The Bluethroat's foods include insects, snails, seeds, and berries. Outside of the breeding season, these birds can be furtive, quiet, and difficult to see.

Bluethroat songs, characteristically delivered from the top of a shrub, are a series of various vocalizations, including buzzes, trills, and shrill sounds. Some begin with crisp, ringing notes, like *tree tree tree tree* or *ting ting ting* or *zri zri zrutt*. Calls include a clipped *tchak* or *track*, a hard *shtick-shtick*, and a sharp *tsee-tchak-tchak*.

SIBERIAN RUBYTHROAT

— Luscinia calliope —

((🐦))
176

A clear, ringing whistle, *ee-uh*, commonly given by this species.

The male Siberian Rubythroat is decorated with the dazzling red throat that gives the species its name, but the female's throat is a plainer, grayish white. These birds are small ground-dwellers with a wide distribution, encompassing much of Asia, including Japan and the Philippines. They are found around bushes, dense undergrowth, and long grass and reeds, often near water. Siberian Rubythroats move about with quick hops and fast, brief runs as they search for insects and seeds. They are known for frequently drooping their wings while they cock their tails upright.

Songs of Siberian Rubythroats usually consist of pleasant, scratchy, warbling notes, which are frequently interwoven with the mimicked vocalizations of other bird species. Calls include a clear, whistled *ee-uh* or *se-ic*, a deep *shuk* or *tschuck*, and a *chack*.

MANGROVE BLUE FLYCATCHER

— Cyornis rufigastra —

((🐦))
177

The male Mangrove Blue Flycatcher uses its song to announce its territory and to attract a mate.

The Mangrove Blue Flycatcher, a relatively little-known species, is an attractive, small bird of Southeast Asia, including the Philippines and Indonesia. In some regions it lives primarily in and around mangroves, near coastal bays and lagoons. Elsewhere the species occupies various other habitats, including forests, forest edges, scrub areas, and even roadside vegetation. Usually alone or in pairs, these little birds forage for insects in the middle and lower parts of mangroves and trees, often searching close to the ground.

Mangrove Blue Flycatchers sing from low perches, often a horizontal branch less than ten feet from the ground. Their sweet-sounding songs generally consist of four to six clear, warbled notes, like *da, de, do, da, der, do*. Calls include a staccato *chik-chik-chik-chik-chik* and a brief *psst* note.

COMMON HILL MYNA

— Gracula religiosa —

((178))

One of the wide variety of calls given by the Common Hill Myna.

The Common Hill Myna is an intriguing bird, celebrated for its ability to mimic the human voice when in captivity. Native to India, southern China, and Southeast Asia, but transported by people fascinated by its vocal mimicry, the species now also lives in the wild in such far-flung outposts as Florida and Puerto Rico. These mynas are active birds that stay in trees of forests and forest edges, occasionally coming down into shrubs to forage. They are gregarious birds, often perching high in trees in pairs or small flocks. Their food consists mainly of fruits and berries, but also some flower buds, nectar, and insects. Larger flocks of Common Hill My-nas sometimes gather at trees that are heavily laden with edible fruit, and forage noisily with other fruit-eaters such as hornbills and barbets.

These mynas have extremely varied vocalizations, including an array of whistles, screeches, wails, and croaks. Their loud, clear, far-carrying notes are often among the dominant sounds of any forest they inhabit. One frequently produced call is a piercing, whistled *ti-ong* or *clee-ong*. Others include a whistle-like *chierk* and a down-slurred *FYEEuw* that sounds something like a falling bombshell.

SPOT-BREASTED LAUGHINGTHRUSH

— Garrulax merulinus —

((🐦))
179

The rich and melodious song of a Spot-breasted Laughingthrush.

The Spot-breasted Laughingthrush is a rather scarce and secretive resident of southern Asia, found from northeastern India eastward into southwestern China and Southeast Asia. It makes its home in forest edges, overgrown clearings, and bamboo thickets. Spot-breasted Laughingthrushes forage on the ground in dense undergrowth, usually in pairs or in groups of up to ten to twenty birds. They hop about, turning over leaves and sticking their bills into nooks and crevices, in search of insects and other small invertebrate animals to eat; they also consume some seeds and fruit.

The vocalizations of this skulking bird have not been extensively studied. However, observers have noted that its songs are rich and melodious, consisting of long, rambling series of clear, musical, whistle-like notes. These songs often contain the mimicked sounds of other birds, including barbets, partridges, and other laughingthrush species. Another vocalization sounds like a coughing chuckle.

SILVER-EARED MESIA

—Leiothrix argentauris —

((🐦))
180

A male Silver-eared Mesia in song.

This stunningly colored little songbird, sometimes called the Silver-eared Leiothrix, is native to the Himalayan region and Southeast Asia, including Myanmar and parts of Indonesia. It resides in forested areas where bushes are plentiful, such as at forest edges and clearings. The Silver-eared Mesia finds its food mainly in bushes, but sometimes in tree canopies as well. In pairs or in groups of thirty or more, these restless birds flit about in foliage, searching for insects and fruit. They commonly associate in foraging flocks with other bird species.

Songs of the Silver-eared Mesia are twangy and cheerful. They consist of repeated, well-spaced whistles or warbles that often descend in pitch, like *che, chu, chiwi, chwu* or *che, tchu-tchu, che-rit*. One long call is a chattering *pe-pe-pe-pe-pe-pe-pe*.

AUSTRALASIA

Many consider traveling to Australasia a journey to the farthest corner of the world; and, with respect to its astonishing birdlife, to the most exotic. The region includes Australia, New Zealand, New Guinea, and several island groups of the southern Pacific. In total, some fifteen hundred bird species inhabit the area, fewer than most other continents. But what this breathtaking region lacks in numbers is more than made up for by its birds' exceptional beauty and amazing behavior.

Australia has about seven hundred forty bird species, a number close to that of the United States or Europe. To mention but a few stand-outs: parrots, including the large and striking cockatoos; the ostrichlike Emu and Southern Cassowary; beautiful bowerbirds that create elaborate stick structures to attract mates; and the megapodes, which construct enormous mounds of decaying vegetation to incubate their eggs.

New Zealand, an island nation located southwest of Australia, has stunning natural scenery. Birdwatchers from around the globe visit to glimpse birds that live nowhere else. These include kiwis, rotund, flightless birds that are the national symbols of New Zealand; the Kea, a particularly curious alpine parrot; and the Rifleman, a tiny insect-eater.

The huge island of New Guinea, located just north of Australia, is best known by birders as home to a great majority of the beautiful birds-of-paradise—tropical wet-forest birds, many with long, elaborate tail feathers or head plumes. Other birds characteristic of the Australasian region are kingfishers, with ten species in Australia, including two kookaburras, and more than twenty species in New Guinea; lyrebirds, which display their spectacular long tails during courtship rituals; fairy wrens, small, colorful birds that usually hold their long tails stiffly upward; and honeyeaters, a group of nectar-eating species.

SOUTHERN CASSOWARY

— Casuarius casuarius —

181

A male Southern Cassowary performs a head throw, while groaning and producing noise with its bill.

The Southern Cassowary is a huge, Ostrich-like bird restricted to the dense rainforests of New Guinea and small portions of northeastern Australia. Undeniably strange-looking with their featherless blue neck, red wattles, and unique bony crest, these impressive birds weigh up to one hundred and twenty pounds. They are found alone, in pairs, or in groups of up to five or six. During the day, these birds spend their time foraging for fruit, which they usually take from the ground after it has fallen; they also eat seeds, mushrooms, and insects and some other small animals. Cassowaries can become quite aggressive during breeding season, defending their young by charging and kicking. The Southern Cassowary is a threatened species in Australia, where habitat destruction and road collisions have decimated populations. The species is still hunted in New Guinea.

Relatively little is known about Southern Cassowary vocalizations. These birds make a variety of sounds, many of them used during breeding. One, probably given by males, is a repeated, deep, loud *boo-boo-boo* or *boom-boom-boom*. Their other calls include grunts, guttural coughs, groans, and hisses, and their threat call is a low rumble or, when very intense, a loud roar.

NORTH ISLAND BROWN KIWI

— Apteryx mantelli —

((🐦))
182

The elusive North Island Brown Kiwi gives nocturnal whistles.

Kiwis, native only to New Zealand, are undoubtedly this island nation's most celebrated animal inhabitants. These fairly large ground birds are active mostly at night, spending the daylight hours asleep in burrows or hollow logs. The North Island Brown Kiwi, restricted to New Zealand's northern main island, lives in forests, shrublands, and agricultural areas. These shaggy-looking, pear-shaped birds emerge at night from their lairs and begin to forage, usually in pairs. They walk along, sniffing loudly; kiwis use their powerful sense of smell to help locate food. Their main prey is earthworms, supplemented by beetles, spiders, crickets, centipedes, and small amounts of seeds, fruits, and leaves. The kiwis plunge their bills deep into the soil to locate food and even dig small holes to extricate particularly large worms.

Kiwis are much more often heard than seen. Their calling, which usually begins right after sunset, is loud and typically shrill. Male North Island Brown Kiwis vocalize more often than females, but the sexes also often duet together. Male calls consist of up to twenty long whistles, each of which may sound like *ah eel*; female calls are more guttural, described as hoarse cries. The species' alarm calls are growling or hissing sounds.

MAGPIE GOOSE

— Anseranas semipalmata —

(((🐦)))
183

Male and female Magpie Geese produce a high-pitched honk.

The Magpie Goose is a very large, lanky, black-and-white goose with a knobbed head. It ranges only over the tropical areas of northern Australia and southern New Guinea, mainly near coasts, and favors wet grasslands and swamps. These geese are usually seen in small to large flocks, grazing on land or feeding in shallow water. Their food consists of seeds, leaves, and roots; the geese dig the latter out of the ground with their hooked bills.

The characteristic vocalization of the Magpie Goose is a fairly high-pitched, resonant honking sound, given in a variety of situations: while flying, while feeding, and even at night. The geese sometimes repeat the honks so rapidly that the sound becomes almost like a trill.

BLACK SWAN

— Cygnus atratus —

((🐦))
184

A mated pair of Black Swans gives several typical calls.

Native swans present a startling sight to birdwatchers and others visiting Australia: In contrast to the swans they are familiar with back home, these swans are almost all black. Black Swans, large birds with wingspans of up to six and a half feet, occur in large lakes, rivers, lagoons, estuaries, and coastal waters. They are seen in pairs, family groups, and in flocks that reach into the thousands. Feeding in the water, flooded fields, or pastures, these stately birds mainly eat the shoots and leaves of aquatic plants, algae, pond weeds, and pasture grasses. Black Swans are also common in New Zealand, where they were introduced.

The most frequently heard call of Black Swans is a melodic bugling, which they produce in flight and also while resting on the water. Other calls include a loud hissing given when defending their nests, and high-pitched whistles.

MICRONESIAN MEGAPODE

— *Megapodius laperouse* —

((🐦))
185

This chickenlike bird produces one of its simple *keek* vocalizations.

Megapodes, or mound-builders, are chickenlike birds that scrape together huge mounds of dirt and vegetation, bury their eggs in the mounds, and then allow the heat of the rotting vegetation to incubate the eggs. Some in the group, such as the Micronesian Megapode, also place their eggs in burrows in the soil or sand and let the sun or geothermal energy warm them. This species, the smallest megapode at about twelve inches long, is found only on the Pacific Ocean islands of the Marianas, including Guam and Saipan, and in Palau. It inhabits mainly patches of forest, but also occurs in coconut groves, coastal scrub, and beachside thickets. Usually noticed foraging in pairs, these megapodes pick from the ground seeds, small fruits, and tiny animals such as spiders, insects, and snails.

Perhaps the Micronesian Megapode's most frequently uttered vocalization is the male's territorial call, given often during early mornings and late afternoons. It begins with a loud *keek* or *skeek* sound that, following a pause, leads to two more *keeks*, often softer. A typical female call starts with a *kek* or *kuk* sound that leads to a long series of louder, rapidly repeated *keek* notes.

WHISTLING FRUIT DOVE

— *Ptilinopus layardi* —

((🐦))
186

The whistle of a male Whistling Fruit Dove, given from the forest canopy.

Fruit doves are a large group of mostly green dove species that have successfully colonized many of the Pacific's small, isolated islands. One of these, the Whistling Fruit Dove, is found only on two of Fiji's small islands, Ono and Kandavu. It prefers forested areas, but is also found in shrublands and occasionally in gardens in local villages. Like most fruit doves, the Whistling Fruit Dove is a tree-dwelling fruit-eater, swallowing small fruits whole. It forages in the middle and lower sections of tree canopies and also lower down, in dense thickets. Males have greenish-yellow heads, but females' heads are a dark olive green.

The glossy green camouflaging plumage of fruit doves renders them difficult to spot in leafy tree canopies, so these birds are far more often heard than seen. Whistling Fruit Dove vocalizations are very unlike the typical cooing calls most people associate with pigeons and doves. Males produce a loud, mellow whistle that rises in pitch, quickly followed by a short, soft trilling sound. Another frequent call consists of a whine and then a squeaky whistle.

NEW ZEALAND KAKA

— *Nestor meridionalis* —

(((🐦)))
187

A New Zealand Kaka gives several vocalizations during the breeding season.

A distinctive rust-red and brown forest parrot, the New Zealand Kaka is found at low and middle elevations on both of New Zealand's main islands. The species has become quite rare in many regions because humans have increasingly altered its forest habitats for development, and its nests are often destroyed by the rats and weasel-like mammals called stoats introduced to New Zealand by people. Kakas are most active in the early morning and late afternoon, when they feed noisily in trees in pairs or groups of up to ten. They are great flyers, often playing, tumbling, and diving in the air above the forest canopy. During the middle of the day, these birds often perch quietly in trees and are typically unseen. Kakas eat kiwi and other fruits, berries, seeds, flowers, buds, nectar, and insects.

New Zealand Kakas are very vocal; observers usually hear their grating calls and whistling notes before they see the birds. They give their most frequently heard vocalizations in flight, including a harsh *kraa-aa* sound and also a warbling or ringing *wheedle wheedle* or *uu-wiiaa* call. Another common call sounds like *choock-choock-choock* or *chok-chok-chok*.

YELLOW-TAILED BLACK COCKATOO
— *Calyptorhynchus funereus* —

((🐦))
188

The squealing flight call of this species sounds like *whee-la*.

The Yellow-tailed Black Cockatoo, a large black parrot, is one of Australia's nine or so cockatoo species. It occurs in the southeastern part of the country and also in the island state of Tasmania, in a variety of habitats, including woodlands and rainforests. Birdwatchers and hikers often spot these birds because they tend to perch at the tops of large trees in open areas, such as clearings and parking lots in national parks. They associate in pairs, small family groups, or, outside of breeding seasons, large flocks. They eat seeds, which they take from the ground or from foliage, and insect larvae. The cockatoos use their powerful bills to strip away bark and dig into the underlying wood to reach the larvae.

Yellow-tailed Black Cockatoos are noisy and conspicuous birds. Their characteristic call, given both in flight and while perched high in trees, is a loud, squealing *whee-la* or *why-lar*. Another common flight call sounds like *keee-ow . . . keee-ow . . . keee-ow*. These birds also make a lot of softer chuckling sounds while flying together in groups, and call in flight just before they land on the trees that serve as night roosts.

LAUGHING KOOKABURRA

— *Dacelo novaeguineae* —

((🐦))
189

A subdued laugh, consisting of repeated *hoo-hoo-hoo* notes, often precedes more intense calling by this familiar species.

After kangaroos and the koala, the Laughing Kookaburra may be Australia's most famous animal resident. Its maniacal laughing call is familiar to many around the world from movies and nature documentaries, even if the particular species that makes the call is less well known. The Laughing Kookaburra occurs naturally in Australia, and via human transport also in parts of New Zealand. The world's largest species of kingfisher, these bulky birds are up to eighteen inches long. These kookaburras inhabit woodlands, forest clearings, parks, orchards, and trees along rivers. They are often spotted in pairs or small groups, perched quietly, looking for prey. They swoop quickly from trees to catch a variety of foods on the ground: earthworms, snails, crabs, spiders, insects, lizards, snakes, and tiny mammals. They also occasionally catch a bug in flight or snatch a fish or frog from shallow water.

The Laughing Kookaburra's celebrated laugh, *koo-hoo-hoo-hoo-hoo-ha-ha-ha-HA-HA-hoo-hoo-hoo*, is a territorial vocalization, given mainly at dawn and dusk. Members of a group often take up the call and answer other kookaburras on nearby territories. This bird's warning call sounds like *kooa*; it also gives screeching calls during fights.

SUPERB LYREBIRD

— Menura novaehollandiae —

((🐦))
190

The song of a male Superb Lyrebird, composed of both original notes and those copied from other species.

Lyrebirds, renowned for their courtship displays, are secretive, pheasant-sized birds that live only in southeastern Australia. The Superb Lyrebird, a resident of temperate rainforests and woodlands, is the larger of two lyre-bird species. During courtship, the male lyrebird displays his spectacular long gaudy tail to females by spreading it and inverting it over his head, then quivering the tail and jumping and spinning about. These birds, which are poor flyers, spend their days on the forest floor but roost in trees at night. When observed, usually as they cross roads or trails, they are alone, in pairs, or in small groups. They forage by walking along and stopping at intervals, using their feet to dig into the soil or tear apart rotting wood in search of worms, spiders, and insects.

The wonderful long songs of Superb Lyrebird males, given often during breeding season and especially during their courtship displays, are famous for including mimicked parts of the vocalizations of other bird species, such as kookaburras and cockatoos. Usually about seventy percent of their vocalizations are imitation. The lyrebirds' own contributions mainly consist of twanging, clicking, and *plikking* notes.

NOISY SCRUBBIRD

— Atrichornis clamosus —

((🐦))
191

A male Noisy Scrubbird's loud song has been described as *chip, chip, chip, chip-ip-ip-ip!*

The Noisy Scrubbird, a small, skulking ground bird, is known for its rarity. It was thought to be extinct until a small population of the species was rediscovered in 1961 in a tiny coastal area of southwestern Australia. This spot is now a protected nature reserve, and the scrubbird is thriving. These fast, alert birds run and creep through the dense under-growth of their favored habitats: thickets, dense scrub, and shrubby forest floors. They poke about in leaf litter, turning pieces over with their bills and snatching mainly insects, but also small lizards and frogs.

Noisy Scrubbirds were named for the males' incredibly loud songs, which can be heard up to a mile away. These songs consist of a series of strident notes, which usually increase in pitch and accelerate until they end abruptly, like *chip, chip chip, chip-ip-ip-ip!*

BROWN TREECREEPER

— Climacteris picumnus —

(((🐦)))
192

The *pink* calls of a Brown Treecreeper, often used to signal mild alarm.

The Brown Treecreeper is a small, stocky forest and woodland bird native to eastern Australia. It is often called "woodpecker" by Australians because it acts somewhat like a woodpecker, foraging on tree trunks, although Australia has no actual woodpecker species. Brown Treecreepers are typically seen alone, in pairs, or in small groups of three to eight. They look for their insect food, chiefly ants and beetles, in trees, poking their slender bills into holes and crevices in trunks and larger branches, and also on the ground.

The Brown Treecreeper's common call is a loud, strident single note, described as *pink*, *weet*, or *spink*. It is uttered singly or rapidly repeated to produce a staccato sound. These *pink*s also signal mild alarm, but when the birds' fear intensifies, the call escalates into a rattling *churr-churr-churr*.

SUPERB FAIRYWREN

— *Malurus cyaneus* —

193

The song of the Superb Fairywren, given by both sexes.

Fairywrens are among the Australian region's most charming and beautiful birds. Outfitted partially in a bright spectrum of blues, these small birds occupy a variety of habitats and often are easy to see in open areas and parks. The Superb Fairywren ranges over much of southeastern Australia, in grassy areas, shrubby parts of forests and woodlands, and also in marshes, riverside thickets, orchards, and gardens. It usually congregates in small family parties that defend communal territories. These groups move quickly through thickets and hop about on grass, foraging for small insects, seeds, flowers, and some fruits. Female Superb Fairywrens have none of the male's glittering blues; their feathers are a mousy brown above and whitish below.

Both sexes of Superb Fairywrens sing, males more often than females. They fly to a shrub-top or fence post and utter an accelerating series of brief, high-pitched notes, *pip pip pip*, which develops into a loud rippling trill. Some observers have likened these songs to the sound produced by a tinny alarm clock. To stay in contact with their group, the birds give calls like *prip-prip*, *scripp-scripp*, or *trrt-trrt*. They emit a sharp *chit* as an alarm call.

RED WATTLEBIRD

— *Anthochaera carunculata* —

((🐦))
194

The Red Wattlebird's song, a raucous, cackling *yakayak*.

The Red Wattlebird, distinguished by the fleshy red wattles that hang below its red eyes, is one of Australia's many species of honeyeaters, birds that specialize in eating plant nectar. It occurs predominantly in forests and woodlands made up of eucalyptus trees, and also in more open areas with trees such as orchards, parks, and gardens. A noisy, aggressive bird, the Red Wattlebird is typically seen in pairs or small flocks, which forage high and low among trees, and occasionally on the ground. They mostly take nectar from eucalyptus flowers, but also some insects from the air. The species ranges over the southern quarter of Australia.

The common vocalization of the Red Wattlebird is a coughlike, raucous cackle, like *yakayak* or *yaak*, *yakyak*. Another frequent utterance is a mellow, whistling *pleu-pleu-pleu* or *tew-tew-tew-tew*.

NOISY MINER

— Manorina melanocephala —

((🐦))
195

The Noisy Miner's common call sounds like the *ping* of a miner's hammer.

If you drive almost anywhere in eastern Australia and pull off the highway to take in a view, the active, quarrelsome birds in the trees nearby are probably Noisy Miners. These grey birds live in open forested and woodland areas, as well as in parks and gardens. They are highly gregarious, associating year-round in groups, usually of five to eight birds. The groups roam circumscribed feeding areas, foraging in tree foliage and on the ground for nectar, insects, and fruits.

The Noisy Miner, as you might expect, is quite vocal; at one time it had the name Garrulous Honeyeater. It gives various loud, penetrating calls; probably the most frequent is one that sounds like *pwee-pwee-pwee* or *tui-tui-tui*. Others are series of repeated *woo* or *wee* notes.

TUI

— Prosthemadera novaeseelandiae —

((🐦))
196

The territorial song of a Tui, a common morning sound in New Zealand.

New Zealand boasts relatively few native songbirds, and many of them are rare and difficult for visitors to see. The Tui, however, is fairly easy to find. It is a blackish bird with an unusual tuft of white feathers at its throat and, in the right light, glossy iridescence. The Tui inhabits chiefly forests and scrub areas, but frequently visits small towns, rural gardens, and suburbs. The Tui is the dominant honeyeater in New Zealand and aggressively chases other Tuis, as well as other nectar-eating birds, away from its feeding areas. Tuis are usually seen solitarily or in small groups, energetically feeding in trees. They prefer to eat nectar, but take fruits and large insects when nectar is scarce.

The Tui is usually one of the first birds heard at dawn in New Zealand. Its songs consist of chains of rich, sweet, pleasant notes, often mixed with various clicks, grunts, gurgles, coughs, croaks and, often, bell-like chimes or bongs. A high-pitched whining sound, *ke-e-e-e*, may serve the species as an alarm call.

EASTERN WHIPBIRD

— Psophodes olivaceus —

((🐦))
197

The whipcrack call of a male Eastern Whipbird gives the bird its name.

The Eastern Whipbird is a striking, crested bird native to Australia's eastern coastal rainforests and moist woodlands, where it is famous for its year-round, deafening whipcrack calls. Whipbirds, which usually associate in mated pairs or small family parties, are terrestrial birds that hop about rapidly through forest undergrowth. They forage on or close to the ground mainly for insects, but also eat some seeds and an occasional small lizard.

Eastern Whipbirds are far more often heard than seen. Pairs call back and forth to each other in brief duets as they forage. The loud, cracking-whip sound is part of the duet: The male utters an introductory note followed by the explosive whipcrack, and the female immediately responds with a quick series of sharp notes, like *choo-choo* or *witch-a-wee* or *awee-awee*. Other calls consist of melodious chuckles and some croaks and clucks.

AUSTRALIAN GOLDEN WHISTLER

— *Pachycephala pectoralis* —

((🐦))
198

An Australian Golden Whistler gives two variations of its song.

Whistlers are small, stout, tree-dwelling songbirds sometimes called thickheads due to their characteristic thick, rounded heads. The Australian Golden Whistler, with its bright yellow coloring, is surely one of the prettiest of the group. It occurs widely over southern and eastern Australia and in New Guinea, inhabiting rainforests, eucalyptus forests and woodlands, and scrub areas. This whistler is usually seen alone or, when breeding, in pairs. The birds tend to stay in tree canopies, hopping rapidly from perch to perch as they search for insects.

The Australian Golden Whistler ranks among the region's outstanding singers. Their songs contain many repeated sweet notes and pure tones and often end sharply, sounding like *choo-choo-choo-choo-chip* and *wheat-wheat-wheat-WHITTLE* and *peep-peep-peep-peep-pu-wit*. The common call is an ascending *seeep*.

RAGGIANA BIRD-OF-PARADISE
— *Paradisaea raggiana* —

((🐦))
199

The courtship vocalizations of a male Raggiana Bird-of-Paradise, used to attract mates.

Birds-of-paradise are undoubtedly among the most exotic and visually stunning of the world's birds. The Raggiana Bird-of-Paradise exemplifies the group with the males' fantastic long reddish plumes and bright patches of yellow and green. Females are plainer and lack the abundant, long plumes. This bird-of-paradise occurs in many parts of New Guinea, mainly in forests at low and middle elevations and other wooded habitats, but it also appears at forest edges and even in gardens. Birds-of-paradise are fruit-eaters, and the Raggiana Bird-of-Paradise takes figs and many other kinds of fruit. It also catches insects on bark surfaces and leaves within the tree canopy.

In addition to their bizarre plumages, birds-of-paradise are celebrated for their courtship displays. Males attract females to communal courting areas called leks with long series of loud, high-pitched notes. When females arrive, the males launch into visual displays to impress them, beating their wings and pumping their heads up and down, calling all the while. Two kinds of longer vocalizations produced by Raggiana Birds-of-Paradise are a series of cries that increase in intensity, *wau wau wau wau wau WAU WAAUU WAAUU WAAAUUU*, and a rapid, high-pitched call, *wok wok wok wak wak wak waagh waagh*.

TOOTH-BILLED BOWERBIRD

— Scenopoeetes dentirostris —

((200))

A portion of the Tooth-billed Bowerbird's diverse repertoire.

Bowerbirds are among the most intriguing birds of all. They build large "bowers," or courtship structures, often from twigs or other plant materials. Males construct the bowers, then show them to females to convince them to mate. The bower of the Tooth-billed Bowerbird is simple: a cleared circular space on the forest floor, which the male has decorated with a few large green leaves. This species, with a notched bill that helps it cut down, rip, and chew leaves, is found only in mountain rainforests in a small corner of northeastern Australia. Tooth-billed Bowerbirds forage in trees and on the ground, alone, in pairs, and sometimes in small groups. They eat fruit and a lot of leaves; small animals such as insects, spiders, and worms form a minor part of their diet.

Tooth-billed Bowerbirds vocalize most during the breeding season. The males' strange songs, which often include mimicked portions of vocalizations of other bird species such as parrots, help attract females to their bower areas. The songs start with soft chuckling notes and then proceed to rich medleys of chatters, chirps, twitters, and whistles. Brief calls include a loud, cheery *chirp* and a low rasp.

ABOUT THE EXPERTS

LES BELETSKY is a professional bird biologist and natural history writer and editor. Prior to taking up nature writing, he conducted twenty years of behavioral research on birds, concentrating on their vocalizations and breeding behavior. He has written or cowritten more than thirty-five papers and four books on birds, one of which won an award from The Wildlife Society as outstanding wildlife ecology book of the year. An avid visitor of bird-watching and wildlife locations across the globe, he has made multiple trips to the Americas, Africa, Asia, and Australia. Detecting a need for comprehensive, single-volume guides for travelers interested in wildlife, he created and edited the *Travellers' Wildlife Guides*, published by Interlink Books (www.interlinkbooks.com). He has written or cowritten twelve of these wildlife travel guides, which illustrate and describe all the kinds of wildlife, birds in particular, that a traveler to a particular state or country might encounter. More about Les Beletsky can be found at www.lesbeletsky.com.

THE CORNELL LAB OF ORNITHOLOGY is a nonprofit institution whose mission is to interpret and conserve the earth's biological diversity through research, education, and citizen science focused on birds. The Lab's Macaulay Library is a major source of sound recordings for research, education, conservation, habitat assessment, the media, and commercial products. Its holdings include more than 160,000 recordings of 67 percent of the world's birds, which have been collected over the eighty years the Library has been operating. It also holds growing numbers of recordings of insect, fish, frog, and mammal sounds. To hear more examples of bird sounds and see dramatic video, visit the online archive at www.animalbehaviorarchive.org.

For more information about The Cornell Lab of Ornithology, including an Online Bird Guide, Citizen Science projects, and authoritative information on birds, visit www.birds.cornell.edu.

ABOUT THE ARTISTS

MIKE LANGMAN left college in 1983 and worked for the Royal Society for the Protection of Birds (RSPB) at their headquarters in Bedfordshire, England, for nine years. His work can be seen at nearly every RSPB nature reserve, including on bird identification posters and large murals in information centers. Mike's illustrations are also used on the RSPB Web site. A full-time bird illustrator since 1992, Mike has worked for many British book publishers, and his work regularly appears in birdwatching magazines in the United Kingdom. He has illustrated eighteen bird books over the last fifteen years, including the Mitchell Beazley *Pocket Guide to Garden Birds*, a series of Hamlyn bird guides, a *Field Guide to the Birds of the Middle East* (T. & A.D. Poyser, 1996), *A Guide to the Birds of South East Asia* (Princeton University Press, 2000), and, most recently, *Bird Songs from Around the World* (Chronicle Books, 2007). The RSPB currently publishes his work in all of their quarterly *Birds* magazines, and he contributes work as voluntary Art Editor for the Devon Birds Society, his local bird organization.

DAVID NURNEY is an experienced bird artist who has traveled to many parts of the world to watch birds. Book credits include: *Bird Songs from Around the World* (Chronicle Books, 2007); *Birds of the World* (Johns Hopkins University Press, 2006); *Bird Songs: 250 North American Birds in Song* (Chronicle Books, 2006); *Nightjars: A Guide to the Nightjars, Nighthawks, and Their Relatives* (Yale University Press, 1998); *Pocket Guide to the Birds of Britain and North-West Europe* (Yale University Press, 1998); and *Woodpeckers: An Identification Guide to the Woodpeckers of the World* (Houghton Mifflin, 1995). He has also contributed illustrated bird plates to the massive and definitive *Handbook of the Birds of the World*.

H. DOUGLAS PRATT is the Curator of Birds at the North Carolina Museum of Natural Sciences. He contributed many plates to *National Geographic*'s best-selling *Field Guide to the Birds of North America* and to the *Handbook of the Birds of the World* series. Other book credits include *Bird Songs: 250 North American Birds in Song* (Chronicle Books, 2006); *The Hawaiian Honeycreepers* (Oxford University Press, 2005); *A Pocket Guide to Hawaii's Birds* (Mutual Publishing, 1996); and *Enjoying Birds in Hawaii* (Mutual Publishing, 1995), among others.

JOHN SILL is an experienced freelance wildlife artist. Book credits include *Bird Songs: 250 North American Birds in Song* (Chronicle Books, 2006); *About Crustaceans: A Guide for Children* (Peachtree Publishers, 2004); *About Insects: A Guide for Children* (Peachtree Publishers, 2000); *Alaska: The Ecotravellers' Wildlife Guide* (Academic Press, 2000); and *Beyond Birdwatching: More Than There Is to Know about Birding* (Peachtree Publishers, 1993), among others.

REFERENCES

Bird names in this book mostly follow those suggested by F. Gill and M. Wright in *Birds of the World: Recommended English Names* (Princeton: Princeton University Press, 2006).

Information on many North American birds comes from *The Birds of North America*, A. Poole, ed. (Ithaca: Cornell Lab of Ornithology).

Beaman, M., and S. Madge. *The Handbook of Bird Identification for Europe and the Western Palearctic*. Princeton: Princeton University Press, 1998.

Beehler, B. M., T. K. Pratt, and D. A. Zimmerman. *Birds of New Guinea*. Princeton: Princeton University Press, 1986.

BirdLife International. *Threatened Birds of the World*. Barcelona and Cambridge: Lynx Editions and BirdLife International, 2000.

Brewer, D. *Wrens, Dippers, and Thrashers*. New Haven: Yale University Press, 2001.

Clement, P. *Thrushes*. Princeton: Princeton University Press, 2000.

del Hoyo, J., A. Elliott, and J. Sargatal (Eds). *Handbook of the Birds of the World, Vol. 7*. Barcelona: Lynx Editions, 2002.

Forshaw, J. M. *Parrots of the World*. Princeton: Princeton University Press, 2006.

Frith, C. B., and B. M. Beehler. *Bird Families of the World: The Birds of Paradise*. Oxford: Oxford University Press, 1998.

Fry, C. H., and S. Keith (Eds). *The Birds of Africa, Vol. VII*. Princeton: Princeton University Press, 2004.

Gibbs, D., E. Barnes, and J. Cox. *Pigeons and Doves: A Guide to the Pigeons and Doves of the World*. New Haven: Yale University Press, 2001.

Grimmet, R., C. Inskipp, and T. Inskipp. *A Guide to the Birds of India, Pakistan, Nepal, Bangladesh, Bhutan, Sri Lanka, and the Maldives*. Princeton: Princeton University Press, 1999.

Heather, B., and H. Robertson. *Field Guide to the Birds of New Zealand*. Oxford: Oxford University Press, 1997.

Howell, S. N. G., and S. Webb. *A Guide to the Birds of Mexico and Northern Central America*. New York: Oxford University Press, 1995.

Jaramillo, A., and P. Burke. *New World Blackbirds*. Princeton: Princeton University Press, 1999.

Jones, D. N., R. W. R. J. Dekker, and C. S. Roselaar. *Bird Families of the World: The Megapodes*. Oxford: Oxford University Press, 1995.

Langrand, O. *Guide to the Birds of Madagascar*. New Haven: Yale University Press, 1990.

Madge, S., and H. Burn. *Crows and Jays*. Princeton: Princeton University Press, 1994.

Mullarney, K., L. Svensson, D. Zetterstrom, and P. J. Grant. *Birds of Europe*. Princeton: Princeton University Press, 1999.

Pizzey, G., and F. Knight. *A Field Guide to the Birds of Australia*. Sydney: HarperCollins Publishers, 1997.

Pratt, H. D. *Bird Families of the World: The Hawaiian Honeycreepers*. Oxford: Oxford University Press, 2005.

Raffaele, H., J. Wiley, O. Garrido, A. Keith, and J. Raffaele. *A Guide to the Birds of the West Indies*. Princeton: Princeton University Press, 1998.

Rassmussen, P. C., and J. C. Anderton. *Birds of South Asia: The Ripley Guide, Vol 2*. Washington D.C. and Barcelona: Smithsonian Institution and Lynx Editions, 2005.

Ridgely, R. S., and J. A. Gwynne. *A Guide to the Birds of Panama*. Princeton: Princeton University Press, 1989.

Ridgely, R. S., and G. Tudor. *The Birds of South America, Vol I*. Austin: University of Texas Press, 1989.

Ridgely, R. S., and G. Tudor. *The Birds of South America, Vol II*. Austin: University of Texas Press, 1994.

Ridgely, R. S., and P. J. Greenfield. *The Birds of Ecuador: Field Guide*. Ithaca: Comstock Publishing, 2001.

Robson, C. *A Guide to the Birds of Southeast Asia*. Princeton: Princeton University Press, 2000.

Sick, H. *Birds in Brazil*. Princeton: Princeton University Press, 1993.

Stevenson, T., and J. Fanshawe. *Field Guide to the Birds of East Africa*. London: T. & A. D. Poyser, 2002.

Stiles, F. G., and A. F. Skutch. *A Field Guide to the Birds of Costa Rica*. Ithaca: Cornell University Press, 1989.

Wells, D. R. *The Birds of the Thai-Malay Peninsula, Vol I*. London: Academic Press, 1999.

CREDITS

ILLUSTRATIONS

Mike Langman: 329, 332, 333, 335, 337, 343, 346, 347, 349, 350, 351, 353, 354, 355, 357, 359, and all chapter opener art, pages 10-11, 190-191, 224-225, 258-259, 292-293, and 326-327.

David Nurney: 18, 21, 23, 37, 43, 45, 51, 55, 61, 69, 71, 73, 79, 81, 84, 85, 87, 89, 90, 91, 93, 95, 97, 101, 103, 105, 109, 117, 119, 121, 123, 125, 130, 135, 137, 143, 144, 104, 147, 153, 157, 159, 161, 165, 172, 175, 181, 189, 193, 194, 195, 197, 199, 201, 202, 203, 205, 207, 209, 211, 212, 213, 214, 215, 217, 219, 221, 223, 227, 228, 229, 231, 233, 235, 237, 238, 239, 241, 243, 244, 245, 247, 248, 249, 251, 253, 255, 257, 261, 262, 263, 265, 267, 269, 271, 273, 275, 277, 279, 280, 281, 282, 283, 285, 287, 288, 289, 291, 295, 297, 299, 301, 303, 305, 307, 309, 311, 313, 314, 315, 317, 318, 319, 320, 321, 323, 324, 325, 331, 339, 341, and 345.

H. Douglas Pratt: 49, 60, 75, 115, and 171.

John Sill: 13, 15, 17, 19, 25, 27, 29, 31, 33, 35, 36, 39, 41, 47, 52, 53, 57, 59, 63, 65, 67, 77, 83, 98, 99, 107, 111, 113, 124, 127, 129, 131, 133, 139, 141, 149, 151, 155, 163, 167, 169, 173, 177, 179, 183, 185, and 187.

AUDIO

Track 001: Steven R. Pantle **002:** William W. H. Gunn **003:** William W. H. Gunn **004:** Curtis A. Marantz **005:** Steven R. Pantle **006:** Paul A. Schwartz, William W. H. Gunn **007:** George B. Reynard **008:** William W. H. Gunn, James M. Hartshorne **009:** George B. Reynard **010:** William W. H. Gunn **011:** William W. H. Gunn **012:** Marian P. McChesney **013:** Gregory F. Budney, Randolph Scott Little **014:** Marian P. McChesney, William W. H. Gunn **015:** Geoffrey A. Keller **016:** Geoffrey A. Keller, David W. Stemple **017:** Andrea L. Priori **018:** Linda R. Macaulay **019:** Oliver H. Hewitt **020:** Arthur A. Allen **021:** Arthur A. Allen, David G. Allen **022:** Arthur A. Allen **023:** Wilber L. Hershberger, George B. Reynard, Randolph Scott Little, Gregory F. Budney **024:** Geoffrey A. Keller, Gregory F. Budney **025:** Geoffrey A. Keller **026:** William W. H. Gunn **027:** Arthur A. Allen, Peter Paul Kellogg, J.P. Meyers, William W. H. Gunn, Mathew D. Medler **028:** Wilber L. Hershberger, Leonard J. Peyton, Randolph Scott Little, J.W. Kimball **029:** Paul A. Schwartz **030:** Stewart D. MacDonald **031:** Arthur A. Allen **032:** Thomas G. Sander **033:** Edgar B. Kincaid **034:** Mark B. Robbins **035:** Charles A. Sutherland **036:** Arthur A. Allen, Peter Paul Kellogg, James L. Gulledge, Gregory F. Budney **037:** Geoffrey A. Keller **038:** Walter A. Thurber **039:** William Guion **040:** Geoffrey A. Keller **041:** Theodore A. Parker III **042:** Gregory F. Budney **043:** Mathew D. Medler **044:** Arthur A. Allen, Peter Paul Kellogg **045:** L. Irby Davis **046:** Gregory F. Budney **047:** Geoffrey A. Keller **048:** Paul A. Schwartz **049:** Geoffrey A. Keller **050:** Geoffrey A. Keller **051:** Geoffrey A. Keller **052:** Geoffrey A. Keller **053:** Geoffrey A. Keller **054:** Geoffrey A. Keller **055:** Geoffrey A. Keller **056:** Geoffrey A. Keller **057:** Geoffrey A. Keller **058:** Geoffrey A. Keller **059:** Geoffrey A. Keller **060:** Geoffrey A. Keller, Gregory F. Budney **061:** Geoffrey A. Keller **062:** Geoffrey A. Keller **063:** Geoffrey A. Keller **064:** Geoffrey A. Keller **065:** Curtis A. Marantz **066:** Randolph Scott Little, Geoffrey A. Keller **067:** Geoffrey A. Keller, Wilber L. Hershberger **068:** L. Irby Davis **069:** Geoffrey A. Keller **070:** Geoffrey A. Keller, Gregory F. Budney **071:** Geoffrey A. Keller, Gregory F. Budney **072:** William W. H. Gunn **073:** William W. H. Gunn **074:** Geoffrey A. Keller **075:** Peter Paul Kellogg **076:** Curtis A. Marantz **077:** Geoffrey A. Keller **078:** Gregory F. Budney, Robert C. Stein **079:** Geoffrey A. Keller, Gregory F. Budney **080:** Geoffrey A. Keller **081:** Geoffrey A. Keller **082:** Chandler S. Robbins **083:** Geoffrey A. Keller, Gregory F. Budney **084:** L. Irby Davis **085:** Mathew D. Medler **086:** Geoffrey A. Keller **087:** William W. H. Gunn, Wilber L. Hershberger **088:** Gregory F. Budney **089:** Steven R. Pantle, Randolph Scott Little **090:** Geoffrey A. Keller, Gregory F. Budney, Robert C. Stein **091:** Gregory F. Budney **092:** Geoffrey A. Keller **093:** Mathew D. Medler **094:** Richard W. Simmers **095:** Geoffrey A. Keller, Randolph Scott Little **096:** Paul A. Schwartz **097:** Randolph Scott Little, William W. H. Gunn **098:** Geoffrey A. Keller **099:** William W. H. Gunn, Bernadette Schrempf **100:** David S. Herr **101:** Theodore A. Parker III **102:** Curtis A. Marantz **103:** William W. H. Gunn **104:** Mathew D. Medler **105:** David Michael **106:** Curtis A. Marantz **107:** William Belton **108:** Linda R. Macaulay **109:** Curtis A. Marantz **110:** Curtis A. Marantz **111:** Curtis A. Marantz **112:** Curtis A. Marantz **113:** Steven R. Pantle **114:** Curtis A. Marantz **115:** Gregory F. Budney **116:** William Belton **117:** Paul A. Schwartz **118:** Paul A. Schwartz **119:** Mathew D. Medler **120:** Myles E. W. North **121:** Myles E. W. North **122:** Myles E. W. North **123:** Myles E. W. North **124:** Myles E. W. North **125:** Myles E. W. North **126:** Myles E. W. North **127:** Clem Haagner **128:** Jennifer F. M. Horne **129:** Linda R. Macaulay **130:** Linda R. Macaulay **131:** Linda R. Macaulay **132:** Myles E. W. North **133:** Ian Sinclair **134:** Jennifer F. M. Horne **135:** Boris N. Veprintsev **136:** Arnoud B. van den Berg **137:** Linda R. Macaulay **138:** Myles E. W. North **139:** Arthur A. Allen, Peter Paul Kellogg **140:** Gregory F. Budney **141:** Gregory F. Budney **142:** Myles E. W. North **143:** Marian P. McChesney **144:** Marian P. McChesney **145:** Myles E. W. North **146:** Scott Connop **147:** Vasily Verschinin **148:** Boris N. Veprintsev, Vladimir V. Leonovich **149:** Boris N. Veprintsev **150:** Vladimir M. Loscot **151:** Boris N. Veprintsev **152:** Vladimir M. Loscot **153:** Wayne W. Hsu **154:** Arnoud B. van den Berg **155:** Scott Connop **156:** Scott Connop **157:** Linda R. Macaulay **158:** Linda R. Macaulay **159:** Sheldon R. Severinghaus **160:** Linda R. Macaulay **161:** Linda R. Macaulay **162:** Geoffrey A. Keller **163:** Edward W. Cronin **164:** Scott Connop **165:** Linda R. Macaulay **166:** Linda R. Macaulay **167:** Joseph T. Marshall **168:** Linda R. Macaulay **169:** Linda R. Macaulay **170:** Linda R. Macaulay **171:** Linda R. Macaulay **172:** Andrea L. Priori **173:** Andrea L. Priori **174:** Gregory F. Budney **175:** Boris N. Veprintsev **176:** Boris N. Veprintsev **177:** Boris N. Veprintsev **178:** Vladimir M. Loscot **179:** William V. Ward **180:** Linda R. Macaulay **181:** Scott Connop **182:** Linda R. Macaulay **183:** Eleanor Brown **184:** Gregory F. Budney **185:** Fred W. Loetscher **186:** Fred W. Loetscher **187:** William V. Ward **188:** William V. Ward **189:** Leslie B. McPherson **190:** Curtis A. Marantz **191:** Linda R. Macaulay **192:** Linda R. Macaulay **193:** Linda R. Macaulay **194:** Curtis A. Marantz **195:** Fred W. Loetscher **196:** H. Douglas Pratt **197:** Kenneth F. Scriven **198:** Fred W. Loetscher **199:** Scott Connop **200:** Scott Connop

INDEX

INDEX

HOW TO USE THE AUDIO PLAYER

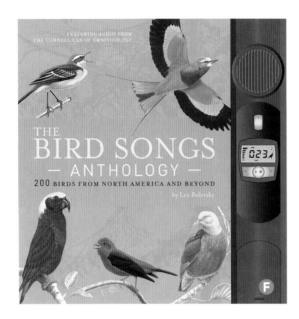 

The 🐦 icons in *The Bird Songs Anthology* are your cue to listen to a bird's song on the attached digital audio player. The number under each icon is the bird song track number.

Press the PLAY button Ⓐ to turn on the audio player. This will activate the LCD screen Ⓑ and display a track number. Press PLAY again to hear this bird's song or use the BACK Ⓒ and FORWARD Ⓓ buttons to select the desired track number. Pressing BACK or FORWARD once will advance the track number display once. Holding down either of these buttons will rapidly scroll through the track numbers.

Pressing the PLAY button while a bird song is in progress will stop the bird song.

Adjust the volume level by pressing + or – Ⓔ. The current volume level is shown on the left side of the LCD screen.

The audio player will automatically shut off after 30 seconds of inactivity. To manually shut off the audio player, hold down the PLAY button for 3 seconds. The audio player will remember the track number and volume level last played.

The audio player includes 3 AAA batteries. To replace the batteries, slide the battery compartment door Ⓕ down.

If you've enjoyed *The Bird Songs Anthology*, you may also be interested in *Bird Songs* and *Bird Songs from Around the World*:

Bird Songs: 250 North American Birds in Song presents the most notable North American birds—including the rediscovered Ivory-billed Woodpecker—in the same book and audio format. Lavish full-color illustrations accompany each account written by bird biologist Les Beletsky, while a sleek, built-in digital audio player holds 250 corresponding songs and calls. In his foreword, North American bird expert and distinguished natural historian Jon L. Dunn shares insights gained from a lifetime of passionate study.

$45.00 ISBN-10: 1-932855-41-6; ISBN-13: 978-1-932855-41-8
Available at your local bookstore or chroniclebooks.com

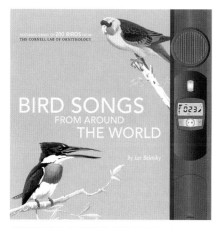

$45.00 ISBN-10: 1-932855-61-0 ISBN-13: 978-1-932855-61-6
Available at your local bookstore or chroniclebooks.com

Bird Songs from Around the World gathers singular birds from six continents. Again drawing from the Cornell Lab of Ornithology's Macaulay Library collection, this book's audio module houses 200 songs from the world's most notable birds, while author and bird biologist Les Beletsky provides a succinct account of each species' distinguishing features and vocalizations. Complete with richly drawn portraits of each bird, plus lavish spreads depicting scenes from each region, this dynamic book brings birds from distant lands to life in your living room.

Praise for the *Bird Songs* series:

"...sweet music for serious birders and wide-eyed amateurs alike."
—*O, The Oprah Magazine*

"...a must-have for your coffee table collection."
—*Denver Post*

"The color illustrations are large and detailed, the text clear and informative..."
—*The Chicago Tribune*

"...a superb sample of the extraordinary variety of bird vocalizations, each one linked to the bird by a concise text and a beautiful painting."
—Rob Hume, Editor, *Birds* magazine

ACKNOWLEDGMENTS

Les Beletsky would like to thank Meghan Cleary, Kate Perry, Henry Quiroga, Leah Finger, and Peter Schumacher of becker&mayer!; Gerrit Vyn and Tammy Bishop of the Macaulay Library of Natural Sounds at the Cornell Lab of Ornithology; David Nurney, John Sill, H. Douglas Pratt, and Mike Langman for contributing the beautiful artwork; David Pearson for his expert ornithological advice; and Cynthia Wang for help with editing.

becker&mayer! would like to thank the many people at the Cornell Lab of Ornithology who provided invaluable assistance. Special thanks to Les Beletsky, Mary Guthrie, and Gerrit Vyn, as well as Daniel Otis, Dana Chiccelley, and Russell Galen.